Slavery, Childhood, and Abolition in Jamaica, 1788–1838

Early American Places is a collaborative project of the University of Georgia Press, New York University Press, Northern Illinois University Press, and the University of Nebraska Press. The series is supported by the Andrew W. Mellon Foundation. For more information, please visit www.earlyamericanplaces.org.

Slavery, Childhood, and Abolition in Jamaica, 1788–1838

COLLEEN A. VASCONCELLOS

The University of Georgia Press
ATHENS AND LONDON

Athens, Georgia 30602
www.ugapress.org

The paper in this book meets the guidelines for permanence and durability of the Committee on Production Guidelines for Book Longevity of the Council on Library Resources.

Most University of Georgia Press titles are available from popular e-book vendors.

Printed in the United States of America
19 18 17 16 15 P 5 4 3 2 1

Library of Congress Control Number: 2015931438
ISBN: 978-0-8203-4802-5 (alk. paper: hardcover)
ISBN: 978-0-8203-4805-6 (alk. paper: paperback)
ISBN: 978-0-8203-4803-2 (e-book)

British Library Cataloging-in-Publication Data available

For Ali, my Jamaican mother, sister, and friend.

Contents

Tables

Acknowledgments

This book has been a long labor of love sixteen years in the making, and it would not have been possible without the many people who helped it come to fruition. First, I want to thank my family for their unconditional love and support. From the childhood vacations spent at historic sites across the eastern seaboard that helped put me on this path to the endless number of phone calls just to say "Hang in there," my parents have been there with me and for me from the beginning. My husband, John, is my foundation, and for that I am so very thankful. Having him in my corner means the world. My sweet friend Alison Delgado, to whom this book is dedicated, has been my guardian angel these past few years. I miss her every day, but I know she would be proud of me as well as this book. Family is strength, and this project is an excellent example of how.

This study would not have been possible without financial support from several institutions. First and foremost, thanks to a substantial Fulbright Fellowship from 2002 to 2003, I was able to spend ten amazing months in Jamaica, where I conducted extensive research in the Jamaican National Archives in Spanishtown, the National Library of Jamaica in Kingston, and the West India Collection at the University of the West Indies in Mona. My time in Jamaica was just as much a life experience as it was a research trip, and I'm so appreciative for the opportunity. I'd like to thank those institutions for allowing me access to the rich sources that they contain, in particular the staff of those institutions, who patiently brought me document after document and who reminded me that I should get something to eat when I forgot (which was more often than not). While there, I had the opportunity to meet Michelle Craig McDonald and Paula Saunders, who were completing their Fulbrights alongside mine, and I valued their input and insight as we worked our way through the material at hand. James Robertson, who was just putting the finishing touches on his impressive study of Spanishtown, Jamaica, was an amazing resource. Not only was his advice on navigating the various collections on the island immensely helpful, but his enthusiastic encouragement of this project was just what I needed on those days when the complexities of the material seemed to dominate the day. Special thanks also to Ken and Isabel Magnus, who welcomed me into their home on several occasions for food, family, and fellowship, as well as the occasional cricket lesson. Short-term grants from the William J. Clements Library at the University of Michigan, the John Hope Franklin Collection at the Duke University Library, and the American Historical Association allowed me to conduct additional research upon my return to the States. I'd like to particularly thank John Harriman, who sadly passed away in 2005, for his assistance at the Clements Library. I'm also grateful to the Graduate School at Florida International University for awarding me the 2003 Dissertation Year Fellowship, a grant that provided immense support during the early writing phase of this book.

I am indebted to many at Florida International University, especially my dissertation committee, for all of the time and effort invested in me during the research, writing, and revision of the original manuscript. My chair, James H. Sweet, who is now at the University of Wisconsin, pushed me to be the historian that I am today, and I hope that I have made him proud. Thanks to his insight and guidance, I was able to write a manuscript that required little revision before its publication, and I thank him for that. I can only hope to be the mentor he was to me to my own students. Sherry Johnson's and Akin Ogundiran's background in Caribbean studies and African history, respectively, helped me to keep this project's focus on the Atlantic, and I so appreciate their comments, suggestions, and encouragement throughout the process. She may not know it, but Sherry's class on Florida and the Caribbean during my first semester in the doctoral program at FIU is what shifted my focus from American history to the Caribbean in the first place, and I am indebted to her for that epiphany. I'd also like to thank Christopher Gray, Alex Lichtenstein, Lara Kriegel, Noble David Cook, Brian Peterson, Victor Uribe-Uran, Ken Lipartito, Anthony Maingot, Darden Pyron, Mark Szuchman, and Sumita Chatterjee, who all offered feedback in one form or another. Thanks especially to Lara Kriegel for valuable feedback on my grant applications and prospectus, Alex Lichtenstein for his direction and encouragement, Noble David Cook for his guidance and magdalena stash, Brian Peterson for making me the teacher I am today, and Anthony Maingot for the valuable conversations on race during my time spent exploring the sociology of slavery. Although I knew him for only a short period of time, Christopher Gray had a massive impact on my research and program of study, and I wish he were around today to see how everything turned out. While at FIU, I had the opportunity of working as a graduate assistant for Sidney Mintz when he joined our faculty as an endowed chair. I so enjoyed our talks and recognize them as a once-in-a-lifetime opportunity to learn from one of the leaders in the field. My Atlantic studies compatriots Audra Diptee, German Palacios, Marcy Duarte, Tom and Penny Cramer, Frank Luca, Jerome Egger, Kindon Meik, and Charlotte Cosner were my FIU family, and our many talks and discussions after class and at conferences were helpful before I hit the archives. Thanks for helping me flush out my ideas so early on. Charlotte and I have always done everything together, from comps to tenure to the publication of our first books, and I've really benefited from the expertise and insight that she's brought to the journey. Last, and certainly not least, I am particularly grateful for Elena Maubrey and Hayat Kassab-Gresham, my Miami mamis, who kept a watchful eye over me during my time at FIU and who sent me love and support while I was researching and writing this manuscript.

Additional guidance, support, and encouragement from friends and colleagues helped that dissertation evolve into the book that it is today. Gary Van Valen, my mentor, colleague, and friend at the University of West Georgia, gave a mountain of advice on the conversion process, and for that I am eternally grateful. Gary, as well as Steve Goodson, Michael de Nie, Aran MacKinnon, Chuck Lipp, and Nadya Williams, all offered excellent feedback and encouragement after I presented my research to them at a departmental talk in 2010. Other members of my department, such as Keith Pacholl, Carrie Pitzulo, Dan Williams, Keith Bohannon, Elaine MacKinnon, and Tim Schroer, have also been equally supportive throughout the process, as has been Emily Hipchen in English. I am lucky to be a member of such a warm group of scholars.

Outside of UWG, I owe a great deal to Mel Page, who first served as my thesis advisor and mentor during my first years of graduate study, and later as my friend. It was his guiding hand that led me to the experiences of children in the transatlantic slave trade, research that would later formulate an early platform for this study. Miriam Foreman-Brunell has also been a huge champion of my work since my first presentation at the Society for the History of Childhood and Youth conference in Washington, DC, in 2000, and I consider myself lucky to have her support and encouragement with this project as well as others. Finally, I would like to thank the University of Georgia Press for giving me the opportunity to publish this book. In particular, I'd like to thank Walter Biggins, who believed in this project and facilitated its publication, as well as the peer reviewers who made detailed comments and suggestions, down to the very mention of specific sources to consult. Thanks to them, this process has been an enjoyable one, and my book is stronger for it. I truly hope that the pages that follow have made it worth their while.

Abbreviations

CL	William L. Clements Library, University of Michigan
DU	Duke University Special Collections Library
IRO	Island Record Office, Spanish Town, Jamaica
JA	Jamaica Archives, Spanish Town, Jamaica
NLJ	National Library of Jamaica, Kingston
PP	British Parliamentary Papers
UWI	University of the West Indies West India Collection, Mona, Jamaica

Slavery, Childhood, and Abolition in Jamaica, 1788–1838

Introduction

In 1745, Governor Edward Trelawny of Jamaica published a controversial pamphlet entitled *An Essay Concerning Slavery.* Much to the consternation of his constituents, he wrote, "I cou'd wish with all my Heart, that Slavery was abolish'd entirely, and I hope in time it may be so." Unlike those who depended on a constant supply of Africans to the island, Governor Trelawny felt that Jamaican planters already owned far too many slaves. Furthermore, they neglected and mismanaged those slaves. Trelawny realized that ending slavery in the colony would bring ruin to an economy dependent on slave-produced sugar, so he simply asked for an abolition of the slave trade and no more. "I shall be content," he wrote, "if no more Slaves be imported, and those we have put under good regulations.—Time will do the rest."[1]

Trelawny's essay did more to annoy Jamaican planters than it did to end the trade to Jamaica. Correspondence and plantation estate books of this early period indicate that Jamaican planters were actually more concerned with production and output than they were with antitrade sentiment. This should not come as a surprise, given the fact that most planters placed profit, investment, and trade at the highest of their priorities. In fact, Jamaica committed 80 percent of its products to international commerce.[2] Furthermore, the island's position as the ostensible jewel in the crown of Britain's sugar economy gave Jamaican planters a strong sense of security, along with the knowledge that British politicians and the West Indian Lobby would protect their most valuable colony at all costs.[3] Consequently, many at home and abroad felt that slavery and the importation of Africans to the island was untouchable. Yet, as Catherine Hall rightly maintains, Jamaica owed its existence to slave-grown sugar, a product that was produced for the mother country; as a result, "successive imperial governments and their colonial officials saw the island through a sugared lens."[4]

The third largest island in the Caribbean, and the largest in the British West Indies, Jamaica supplied 54 percent of all tropical imports to Great Britain and 13 percent of the empire's total imports by 1750.[5] That year, Jamaica was worth over £10 million sterling, a number that catapulted to over £28 million sterling by 1774.[6] By 1805, the island exported nearly 100,000 tons of sugar, surpassing any other country in the world, and just five years later it became the world leader in coffee exports.[7] During that time, the island experienced massive economic expansion, undoubtedly in response to increased demands overseas, nearly doubling the number of sugar estates on the island to well over a thousand by the end of the eighteenth century.[8] According to Trevor Burnard, Jamaica's slave-owning elite became the wealthiest men in the British Empire, thereby making the island Great Britain's wealthiest colony.[9]

For a white population that constituted only 9 percent of the 142,000 who lived on the island in 1750, amassing such wealth was indeed impressive.[10] Aside from the fact that mortality among whites was extremely high, the majority of Jamaica's planter elite preferred to maintain residency in Britain as absentee planters. As Vincent Brown illustrates in his book *The Reaper's Garden*, life expectancy for whites living on the island equaled that of whites living in West Africa, where nearly 60 percent died within their first year of residency.[11] Burnard, who has characterized the colony as nothing more than a "white man's graveyard," argues that European immigrants to Jamaica lived only an average of twelve years after their arrival.[12] Despite the fact that 40 percent of England's West Indian colonists lived on the island, the white population remained a significant demographic minority for the entire period of this study, an issue that came to be quite a concern for those few whites living in Jamaica, so much so that the Jamaican Assembly created the Deficiency Acts in order to stop the popular practice of absenteeism on the island.[13] By 1830, only about one third of Jamaica's planters were residents of the island.[14]

It is important, though, to recognize and acknowledge that without the presence of chattel slavery, Jamaica would have been just a tropical island sitting ninety miles from Spanish Cuba. These sugar barons were absolutely dependent upon their enslaved laborers, despite that strong sense of security regarding their high place in Britain's economy. In fact, they never could have amassed such wealth without them. From 1655 to 1808, Jamaica imported an estimated 701,046 Africans to the island, with an estimated 605,000 of that number arriving from 1750 to 1808 alone.[15] During the years of the legal trade, an island just 150 miles wide purchased one third of the enslaved Africans shipped to the British West Indies.[16] Sixty percent of those enslaved men, women, and children toiled on sugar plantations on holdings averaging between three hundred and five hundred slaves.[17]

Consequently, the island's enslaved population never increased by natural means, and enslaved Africans died in alarming numbers within their first three years on the island.[18] Jamaica's enslaved Creoles, those of African descent born into slavery on the island, had a much higher life expectancy; most could expect to live anywhere from twenty to thirty years.[19] In 1754, an estimated 130,000 slaves lived in Jamaica; by 1808 that number had risen to an estimated 324,000.[20] While that may seem like an impressive population increase over thirty-four years, any rise in the enslaved population likely came from purchase rather than natural increase, as Jamaican planters long ascribed to the belief that it was much cheaper to buy Africans at market than to breed their own slaves. In fact, most planters discouraged their female slaves from becoming pregnant during these early years. Not only did pregnancy reduce productivity, but planters and estate managers were reluctant to lose enslaved women in childbirth. Instead planters felt it more rational to use their enslaved women to their full potential as field laborers, an easily replaceable commodity in this early period.

Everything changed in 1783, however, when the Quakers presented Parliament with the first petition to abolish the transatlantic slave trade. As petitions like these increased in number and strength over the following years, Jamaican planters gradually comprehended that their labor supply was in danger. Consequently, they asked themselves, "If Great Britain was to give up the Slave Trade, what would be the consequence?"[21] For an island that relied so heavily on the importation of Africans to replenish the labor supply, that earlier sense of security that Jamaican planters felt began to falter. Furthermore, it was no secret that staunch abolitionists like William Wilberforce, Thomas Clarkson, and Hannah More intended to set their sights on ending slavery itself; however, they needed to abolish the slave trade first. Needless to say, Jamaican planters and the West Indian Lobby began to feel more insecure with each submitted petition.[22]

As a result, all parties involved began to look more closely at the situation at hand. After a series of investigations and inquiries beginning in 1788, the Jamaican Assembly concluded that the enslaved population could not possibly sustain itself with "the disproportion of the sexes" aboard ship and on Jamaican plantations, a situation exacerbated by the high mortality rate among the newly imported.[23] While the Assembly claimed that Jamaica annually imported three females to every five males, Stephen Fuller, agent for Jamaica, reported that out of the 250,000 slaves on the island, males outnumbered females by thirty thousand.[24] As Fuller warned that the gender imbalance was of great importance to Jamaica's place as a leading contributor to Britain's economy, many planters opted to buy more African "breeding wenches" and young girls in the hopes of evening out the disproportion between the sexes on their estates.[25] Any doubts planters had about the seriousness of the situation quickly faded in April 1792, when the House of Commons voted by a large majority to gradually abolish the British slave trade. Insecurity turned into panic when the House voted a few weeks later to end the trade by January 1, 1796. Neither of these resolutions passed the House of Lords, who obviously sided with the West Indian Lobby.[26] None of that mattered to the Jamaican planters, who were forced to begin imagining a future without African imports.

What becomes clear is that Jamaican planters came to depend on youth and childhood, just as they were economically dependent on the slave trade. Before any threats to the trade, planters throughout the Americas saw Africans as an easily replaceable commodity. They could and would work their slaves to death with the knowledge that there would always be another trade ship on the horizon with fresh laborers in their cargo holds. Once abolitionists became more powerful in Parliament, however, that endless supply of labor became increasingly more threatened. Consequently, Jamaican planters gradually adopted the strategy of importing younger slaves into the island, and youth quickly became an attractive asset on the auction blocks of the Jamaican slave markets.[27] That is how abolitionist sentiment changed eighteenth-century definitions of risk, investment, and profit. As Jamaican planters increasingly purchased more (and younger) breeding wenches, laws like the Dolben's Act of 1788 also led to the presence of younger African boys on British ships.[28] Planters, the West Indian Lobby, politicians, and traders all began to modify their ideas of profit and risk, as well as their ideas of child worth, throughout the Atlantic world. Simply put, they came to believe that youth and childhood would lead them out of the inevitable.

As we will see, however, Jamaican planters also revisited the idea of childhood as it related to plantation management and profit during this period. According to one planter, "The care of Negroes, the causes of increase and decrease, &c., &c., are becoming the subject of common conversation among a description of persons who used only to think of the speediest methods of obtaining labors."[29] The assemblymen who had once scoffed at the controversial ideas of Governor Trelawny began taking measures to ameliorate the condition of their slaves in order to invest in the natural increase possibilities of the enslaved Africans and Creoles they already owned. In the pages that follow, we will see how these changes and ameliorative measures affected not only the definition and nature of childhood in Jamaica but also the very lives of the children already living on Jamaica's estates.

The Historiography

Today when one thinks of the historiography surrounding abolitionism, one is immediately drawn to the now famous Williams Thesis and the debates that followed.[30] These groundbreaking debates forced students and historians of slavery to question the complicated relationship between the Enlightenment, capitalism, and Britain's antislavery movement. Yet, the conversation that ensued examined this relationship largely through political and economic lenses. What participants failed to consider, however, was how this decision process impacted those who were the object of the discussion—especially the children of slaves.

It is not surprising that children did not enter the debate until now, as children traditionally find themselves on the fringes of historical discourse. Until recently, slave studies rarely discussed children's experiences as slaves. Gilberto Freyre was the first to examine enslaved children in his book *The Masters and the Slaves* (1945). Devoting two chapters to slave childhood as part of a much larger examination of planter-slave relationships in colonial Brazil, Freyre briefly discusses the complicated relationships between slave mother and child, as well as the difficult relationships between white and enslaved children. While showing that enslaved children suffered physically as slaves to the same degree as adults, Freyre argues that the realization that they were nothing more than chattel or a toy for cruel white children damaged enslaved children psychologically. What resulted was something that Wilma King would later call a "stolen childhood."[31]

With the publication of two important works on child slavery in the antebellum South by King and Marie Jenkins Schwartz, the study of slave childhood has emerged as a serious field of scholarly inquiry. In *Stolen Childhood* King argues that enslaved children in the antebellum South suffered a stolen childhood immediately after entering the workforce in their quick passage from child to adult slave. Their life outside the workforce failed to prepare enslaved children for the hard labor, harsh treatment, and familial separation they experienced to much greater degrees while working as field and domestic laborers. Therefore, their experiences as children forced them to grow into adulthood well before their time.[32] In *Born in Bondage* Schwartz contends that slave childhood was more contested than stolen as mothers struggled with planters over the control of their child's upbringing. Although she concurs that planters interfered with every aspect of slave life, Schwartz moves away from King's argument to show how the slave community fought against such interference and often gained the opportunity to raise their children as they saw fit.[33] Schwartz recognizes that slaves were not powerless in their child-rearing practices or their influence on their own children. Although neither historian focuses on how childhood changed over time, their different approaches center on various stages of childhood. While King takes a more thematic approach by examining the stages of slave childhood from the perspectives of family, leisure and play, work expectations, and spirituality, Schwartz examines her subjects from a developmental point of view, acknowledging their progression from birth to early childhood to adolescence and finally adulthood. While these two works are the most extensive examinations of slave childhood to date, both present static and homogenized histories that fail to examine how the idea of childhood changed over time, and neither considers how the abolitionist movement affected or impacted children's experiences as slaves.

Despite these new strides in the field of American history, Caribbean slave studies continue to examine slave childhood as part of a much larger discussion of slavery. Although those works that followed *The Masters and the Slaves* move away from Freyre's paternalistic viewpoint, they merely place children in much larger examinations of gender or family in the plantation complex. Historians such as Barbara Bush, Richard Sheridan, Kenneth Kiple, and Richard Steckel take an epidemiological approach while discussing how an enslaved mother's workload, malnutrition, and harsh treatment contributed to the astounding infant and child mortality rates within the slave community.[34] Bush, along with other Caribbeanists such as Marietta Morrissey, Lucille Mathurin Mair, and Hilary Beckles, also examines slave childhood in relation to the complexities of mother-child relationships in much larger discussions of gender and slavery in the British Caribbean.[35]

Barry Higman and Elsa Goveia were the first Caribbeanists to touch on issues more directly related to slave childhood in their studies of slave family in the Caribbean by deviating from the traditional historiographical trends in order to examine the social environments in which enslaved children lived.[36] While Higman's more quantitative and archaeological examinations of the Jamaican slave villages argues that enslaved children largely lived in nuclear families, Goveia stresses the presence of matrifocal families composed strictly of a woman and her children. Both historians, however, oversimplify the idea of family in the slave community by failing to realize the more complex formations of reinvented kinship groups, families with adopted children, and the presence of orphans in the slave villages. Despite these valuable contributions to the current historiography, none of these works examines the experiences of children apart from these issues. Furthermore, they all fail to discuss how childhood in the slave community changed over time or even how the growing abolitionist movement unfolding in Europe affected children's lives.

The unpublished thesis of Beverley Blake is the first study to specifically focus on the changing nature of childhood in Jamaica, though she only briefly examines enslaved children as part of a larger discussion of child rearing and child socialization in nineteenth-century Jamaica.[37] Furthermore, although she acknowledges change over time, with economic and political factors being the main catalysts, her discussion of slave childhood shows minimal change at best. In other words, Blake asserts that the only change really taking place for enslaved children in the nineteenth century was their acquisition of freedom after apprenticeship.

An Overview

This study moves beyond the current historiography to discuss the nature of child development in the plantation complex, how colonial Jamaican society and the slave community defined childhood, and how that definition changed over time. I build on the existing literature not only by discussing slave childhood as a separate entity from other issues, such as family, gender, and even childhood in general, but also by demonstrating that slave childhood was not a static entity during my period of study. The abolitionist movement and Jamaican planter reactions to that movement played an important part in the ever changing state of childhood within the slave community. By the mid-eighteenth century, Jamaica had replaced Barbados as the most favored and most important British colonial possession. As such, the island possessed the largest enslaved population in the entire British Caribbean by 1750. This study examines childhood and slavery in Jamaica from the beginnings of amelioration in 1788 to the eventual end of Jamaican slavery and apprenticeship in 1838. By focusing specifically on the changing nature of slave childhood in Jamaica during this period, I show how childhood and slavery influenced and changed each other throughout this period, during which the abolitionist movement was the main catalyst for change.

I see these changes taking place through several shifts in planter ideas about childhood. Before 1788, when the abolitionist cause was in its infancy, the island's planters disregarded and discouraged the presence of enslaved children on their estates. Abolitionist sentiment against the transatlantic slave trade gained momentum as well as support from Parliament beginning in the 1750s, and in 1788 Jamaican planters began to apply a program of amelioration within their slave management practices as a direct response. That said, this is also a study of amelioration and how those policies and practices related to the changing nature of childhood within the slave community. As part and parcel of their ameliorative strategies, we see Jamaican planters and plantation managers gradually shifting their stance on enslaved children by not only openly encouraging slave births but also by passing the first laws rewarding natural increase.

As the colony's planters became increasingly convinced that Jamaica could not continue as a slave society without the presence of enslaved children on their estates leading them toward the security they once enjoyed, ameliorative measures on the island intensified and planter importation preferences changed after 1788. Therefore, in the years prior to the abolition of the slave trade in 1808, ideas of child worth and value also shifted as planters realized the need for change in the management and treatment of the women and children on their estates. The lives of enslaved children reflected these changes for the better in medical, social, and quantitative terms. Between 1815 and 1834, planter opinion shifted slightly as abolitionist sentiment shifted its attentions to the dissolution of slavery itself. As a result, Jamaican planters came to value enslaved children as both economic and social investments and began to socially condition the enslaved population into a more manageable class of people by impressing Christian and English values upon the enslaved children on their estates. By 1834, planter opinion had shifted yet again, as the abolitionists succeeded in their goal of ending slavery in all British dominions after a brief apprenticeship period. Between 1834 and 1838, therefore, enslaved children shifted from investments back to liabilities. As the planter elite redefined the place of childhood and youth on their estates, many came to view enslaved children as the one thing that would save Jamaica from economic collapse.

Within this discussion on the changing nature of childhood in Jamaican slave society, two key questions remain central: What is a child, and how does that definition change over time? Based on their labor expectations, Jamaican planters, estate managers, bookkeepers, and overseers designated slaves age fifteen and younger as children. While children joined the ranks of the plantation labor force between the ages of five and six, they largely did not begin working in the same labor gangs as adult slaves until the age of sixteen. As enslaved children transitioned from nursery to field, and from gang to gang, the tasks they performed were designed to progressively socialize and acclimate them to their lives as chattel. Consequently, the nature of their work played a heavy role in defining the stages of their childhood.

In fact, the complex triangle of growing abolitionist sentiment, the plantation economy, and the changing nature of work on Jamaica's estates influenced and altered slave childhood throughout this period. As abolitionist sentiment gained both momentum and strength, the white community assigned ever changing subcategories to childhood based on the perceived value, need, and place of enslaved children in the system. As the characterization of childhood expanded beyond the limitations of labor expectations, terms such as *infant*, *boy*, *girl*, *man-boy*, and *woman-girl* complicated planter definitions of slave childhood. This was especially true as more and more enslaved girls became known as *breeding wenches*. These subdivisions generated a more complex definition of childhood that increasingly came into accord with European definitions of the term.

In other words, planters began to apply the term *childhood* to the slave community for the first time. Not only were they taking these new definitions seriously, but planters were taking enslaved children seriously as well. While an infant could be a child below the age of two, some bookkeepers used the term to describe all children of nonworking age on the estate. The terms *man-boy* and *woman-girl*, identifiers that grew out of the demands of the slave trade, usually applied to adolescents between the ages of sixteen and eighteen. Later, when children became more important to the struggle against natural decrease on the island, the term *women-girls* occasionally referred to pubescent girls below the age of sixteen. Furthermore, ideas of womanhood occasionally stretched to girls as young as ten, who were raped by the white men on their estates. In fact, the nature of girls' work became more complex as planters increasingly linked gender to reproductive potential, and enslaved girls' work summarily took on a reproductive component as a result. By the time enslaved girls reached the delicate age of eleven, they were women; more specifically they were breeding wenches. Therefore, ideas of childhood were not only changing, but they were subjective as well.

This is not to say that this is primarily a study of slave childhood from a planter point of view. Abolitionism merely provides the best opportunity to see how slave childhood changed over time. In addition to highlighting how the abolitionist movement, as well as planter responses to that movement, changed the nature of childhood in Jamaica, this study reveals how these changes affected the quality of life for Jamaican enslaved children. Although I take a chronological approach, it is through a topical presentation that I am able to give these children, and especially their mothers, a voice. With each chapter focusing on a different aspect of the slave experience, I examine a childhood defined by planter opinion and manipulation and affected by the institution of slavery itself.

As would be expected, source material for this project was elusive. The quantity and quality of my evidence suffers from gaps in documentation, age, and environmental deterioration. In addition, because most slaves were illiterate, only a minute fraction put their memories to paper, and those accounts were influenced by the abolitionist movement of the eighteenth and nineteenth century. Consequently, the majority of my sources are from the planters' point of view.

Despite these challenges, I was able to dissect the experiences of Jamaican enslaved children in order to give them a voice alongside that of their owners. I consulted a wide variety of sources that enabled me to reveal a slave perspective. Personal memoirs, diaries, travel accounts, and private correspondence were especially useful as their observations occasionally shed light on the actions and feelings of the slave community. The two best examples are the diaries of Thomas Thistlewood and the journal of Matthew "Monk" Lewis, as these two slave owners often took the time to carry on conversations with their slaves. Although sources like these reveal changes in planter opinion toward enslaved children in Jamaica, their candid accounts bring to light much about how the planters viewed their slaves and add insight into how the slaves themselves viewed their situation. For example, while Thistlewood discusses the random acts of theft and vandalism committed by children on his estates, Lewis describes in great detail the development of miscegenation in Jamaica as well as the slave community's social stratification of the children who resulted from such unions.

While contemporary accounts provide valuable insights into planters' opinions, local administrative and court proceedings that are available only in Jamaica allowed me to gain a better understanding of Jamaican slave childhood from the perspective of the slaves themselves. Archival sources such as Slave Court records as well as the Special Magistrate proceedings under apprenticeship were vital to this discussion, as they demonstrate how children and their mothers reacted to their situation as slaves and later as apprentices. These records show the frequent acts of theft, violence, vandalism, and marronage committed by women and children, yet the courts were one of the few venues where slaves and apprentices could voice their opinions and feelings about the institution of slavery and its abolition. Furthermore, these records allow us to better see the harsh conditions of slavery and apprenticeship outside of the planter point of view, as these sources often record the grievances and complaints of parents and children in the slave and apprenticed communities. Other sources, such as the Registry of the Returns of Slaves (1817–32) and various plantation and estate inventories, occasionally list valuable information in the form of brief descriptions or records of Creole children with African names, familial formations, or acts of infanticide and child murder.

Sources such as the Jamaican Assembly journals and votes, as well as the Laws of Jamaica, show how planter opinion changed toward the idea of slave childhood. While these sources are extremely useful in terms of gauging planter frustration and desperation with the rise of abolitionist sentiment in England, they rarely give enslaved Jamaicans a voice. Other sources provide quantitative data, such as the Registry of the Returns of Slaves and various plantation and estate inventories. Although these sources are particularly useful when examining the nature of the slave increase and decrease under amelioration, they offer little insight into children's experiences as slaves. I carefully gleaned this information from planters' memoirs, letters, and diaries.

I begin by analyzing the experiences of enslaved children as laborers on the island's plantations and estates before and after the amelioration laws of 1788 and the abolition of the slave trade in 1808. As planters placed more and more responsibility on enslaved children to lead them toward the economic stability and profitability they desired, their interference and manipulation had damaging physiological and psychological effects on the children's already fragile psyches. Although I concur with Wilma King's argument that a shortened childhood forced enslaved children into adulthood before their time, I also demonstrate that slave childhood in Jamaica was a contested process that changed with each generation of children.[38] Chapter 1 expands on past arguments concerning childhood under slavery, delving deeper into these issues by showing how children reacted to their situation as slaves through acts of resistance, violence, and crime. I examine their lives outside of slavery as well by building on previous discussions of mother-child relationships, child-rearing practices, and ideas of family in the slave community put forth by historians such as Bush, Morrissey, and Higman. This allows me to visualize how enslaved children coped with the hardships of slavery—such as death, familial separation, and immense poverty—as many children reinvented and modified their ideas of family and kinship in order to survive their situation.

Chapter 2 continues this discussion on the changing nature of childhood in Jamaica through the lens of race by investigating the life experiences of mulatto children and their relationship to the whites who fathered them. As a result, I am able to juxtapose slave family and childhood against a new examination of miscegenation, social stratification, and manumission. While I argue that their whiteness often elevated the status of enslaved mulatto children on the island, that whiteness actually diminished their value to the Jamaican plantation economy. Despite their limited worth to Jamaican planters, I show that their existence complicated the idea of childhood held by most planters by forcing white society to recognize and gradually accept their identity as children apart from their identity as slaves.

The last two chapters focus on education and ideas of freedom as they developed in the slave community. Chapter 3 places enslaved children in the context of the ethnic diversity of the slave community and how the variety of cultural traditions and beliefs such as folklore, naming practices, and language present on the island specifically related to children within the slave community. The slave community thus had many opportunities to raise their children on their own terms. Once abolitionist sentiment focused on the institution of slavery itself, however, enslaved parents struggled to maintain control over the education of their children as planters attempted to change the nature of African cultural identity by impressing Christian and English values on the enslaved children in Jamaica as well as their kinship groups.

This discussion is continued in chapter 4 as part of a larger discussion on the apprenticeship period. It is also in this chapter that we see planter ideas of childhood come full circle, with abolition serving as the main catalyst for change once again. As planters shifted from slave to free labor during the apprenticeship period, children shifted from investment to liability overnight. Yet, just as planters devalued the children on their estates, the abolition of slavery in Jamaica enables us to see the value the former slave community placed on these children as they demanded and often received a negotiated freedom for their children during this transitional period. Although childhood returns to its previous status as a liability in the eyes of the Jamaican planters, I argue that Jamaican children faced the prospect of an undefined childhood after apprenticeship, one that was free from planter control and gave Jamaican laborers as a whole a newfound hope for the future.

I should stress that this is not a study of the slave trade, the English abolitionist movement, or the planter class in Jamaica. Nor is it a study of urban slavery, slave family, gender, or race. These are important topics that I touched on and may expand on later, but they are not my primary concern in the pages that follow. Although each chapter discusses changes in slave childhood from a planter point of view, by exploring children's experiences as slaves through the lenses of family, resistance, race, status, culture, education, and freedom, this study attempts to give slave children a voice by examining how they carved a place for themselves in the slave community. In doing so, I reveal a great deal about slave family and childhood from the inside. Furthermore, I depart from the static examinations of the past in order to reveal more textured, complex, and succinct explanations of how slave childhood progressed and changed throughout my period of study, and I add a social dimension to past and current debates on abolition that fail to include the slaves themselves. In the end, this study tells the story of an overlooked childhood, one that was often defined by Jamaican planters but always contested and redefined by the slaves themselves.

1 / "To so dark a destiny My lovely babe I've borne": Slavery and Childhood in Jamaica in the Age of Abolition

In his controversial pamphlet entitled *An Essay Concerning Slavery*, Governor Edward Trelawny wrote in 1745, "It is notorious that in most Plantations more die than are born there." To illustrate his point he created a fictional dialogue between an officer and a Jamaican planter in which he alleged that harsh treatment, miscarriages, abortions, and promiscuity contributed to the infertility of the enslaved population. While the planter lamented the failure of his estate to increase naturally, the officer offered him insight and advice: "If a little Linnen, or other Necessaries, were given to every Wench that was brought to Bed, and all the barren ones whipt on a certain Day every Year, I fancy the Negroe Ladies would yield better, and at least keep up the present Stock."[1]

In Trelawny's opinion, one that many in his station did not share, Jamaican planters already owned far too many slaves. Furthermore, they neglected and mismanaged their slaves, which provided the impetus for his uncharacteristic plea. Much to the consternation of his constituents, he wrote, "I cou'd wish with all my Heart, that Slavery was abolish'd entirely, and I hope in time it may be so." Yet, Trelawny realized that ending slavery in the colony would bring ruin to an economy dependent on slave-produced sugar, so he simply asked for abolition of the slave trade and no more: "I shall be content if no more Slaves be imported, and those we have put under good regulations.,—Time will do the rest."[2]

As did his thoughts on ending the trade, it is not surprising that Trelawny's ideas about ameliorating the condition of Jamaica's slaves fell on deaf ears as well. Although the enslaved population failed to reproduce naturally, Jamaican planters preferred to purchase slaves directly from Africa rather than invest time and money in children who most likely would never reach their full work potential as adults. Once abolitionist threats to the slave trade intensified, however, Jamaican planters gradually acknowledged the value of enslaved children and took stock in Trelawny's words of warning. In this chapter, I analyze how these changes affected the nature of Jamaican slavery and slave childhood throughout my period of study. By examining slave childhood before and after the abolition of the slave trade, I will consider how these children developed physically and psychologically in the plantation complex. After briefly discussing the development of pro-natal policies during the late eighteenth and early nineteenth centuries, I will analyze the outcome of Jamaica's amelioration policies on the natural increase of the enslaved population. Once British abolitionists succeeded in ending the trade and switched their attention to the institution of slavery itself, enslaved children became more important commodities in Jamaica.

Mortality and Planter Opinion in Early Eighteenth-Century Jamaica

Until the mid-eighteenth century, children were unwanted chattels on Jamaican estates and planters largely discouraged their female slaves from becoming pregnant. "I am aware that there are many planters who do not wish their women to breed," William Beckford, a prominent Jamaican planter, wrote in 1788, "as there by so much work is lost in their attendance on their infants."[3] It really is no surprise that slave owners felt this way. When even the white population did not increase demographically in this "white man's graveyard," why would plantation owners and managers have any reason to believe that natural increase among the enslaved population was ever likely?[4] Not only did pregnancy reduce productivity, but planters and estate managers were reluctant to lose enslaved women in childbirth. Instead they felt it more rational to use their enslaved women to their full potential as field laborers, an easily replaceable commodity in this early period. Furthermore, the majority of Jamaica's enslaved children did not begin work in the labor gangs until at least age five, and then they performed only minor tasks until they joined the first gang in their adolescence. Therefore, planters generally viewed those few children on their estates as financial burdens since they had to be supported without any reciprocal contribution to the plantation economy.

While Jamaican planters and estate managers discouraged enslaved women from having children, the hard labor, harsh treatment, and low birth rates endemic on the plantations made any natural increase impossible. James Ramsay, who witnessed slave life on British West Indian plantations firsthand for twenty years, wrote in 1784, "It is not an unusual thing to lose in one year . . . ten, twelve, nay, as far as twenty, by fevers, fluxes, dropsies, the effect of too much work, and too little food and care."[5] Archival evidence supports Ramsay's claims, showing that any increase on the island's estates came largely from the purchase of Africans imported to the island.[6] Although thirty-five children were born on Spring Vale Pen in the parish of St. James between 1791 and 1800, forty-eight slaves died, motivating the purchase of seventy Africans during this nine-year period.[7] Worthy Park Estate in St. Catherine is an even better example: forty-eight children were born on the estate from 1792 to 1796, but 137 slaves died. Yet, despite this natural decrease, Worthy Park's enslaved population increased from 357 slaves in 1792 to 470 slaves in 1796.[8] Unfortunately, figures such as these are unavailable for other Jamaican plantations, as bookkeepers annually recorded only the overall number of slaves on their estates, indicating that estate managers and bookkeepers cared little about the birth and death of enslaved children. Records like these offer little insight into the nature of childbirth or infant and child mortality on Jamaican estates during these early years.

Despite minimal quantitative evidence, we do know that very few children during this early period were strong enough at birth to survive even the first few months of life. Life on a Jamaican plantation was incredibly hard for enslaved women and took a devastating toll on their bodies. Pregnant or not, enslaved women worked an average of twelve hours each day in the fields, sharing the same difficult labor as enslaved men. Others performed backbreaking labor as washerwomen, weavers, and water carriers either on Jamaican estates or in the urban areas.[9] Whether working in the fields or as domestics, enslaved women suffered from the general weakness and frailty associated with an inadequate and vitamin-deficient diet, little or no prenatal care, excessive exertion, and Draconian physical abuse. Pregnancy and childbirth did not guarantee immunity from their plantation duties, and most enslaved women worked until a few days before their due dates only to return to work a few days after giving birth.[10] Others gave birth in the fields, as was the case with Ellen, a woman belonging to Egypt Estate in Westmoreland. In September 1759, the estate overseer Thomas Thistlewood noted that Ellen's child died from "the hurt it rec'd When it fell from her."[11]

Pregnancy did not guarantee immunity from harsh punishment, and it was not until the last years of slavery that Jamaican law lightened punishments and prohibited the flogging of enslaved women.[12]

The absence of pro-natal policies, adequate medical care, work reduction, and a nutritional diet all worked against pregnant slaves and their unborn children. Some women died in childbirth or soon after; others miscarried or were forced into an early labor, only to give birth to stillborn children. Michael Craton and Kenneth Morgan have both estimated that only 1 out of every 4.6 children born to enslaved women in Jamaica were live births.[13] Most enslaved women who experienced successful births delivered severely malnourished and unhealthy children with little chance of survival. According to Barry Higman, as many as 50 percent of all children born during this period died in the first nine days of life.[14] More recent figures by Morgan show an 80 percent mortality rate among newborns during the first two weeks of life in the eighteenth century, dropping to 50 percent in the nineteenth century.[15] Breastfeeding did little to alleviate the situation, as enslaved children fed only on vitamin-deficient milk for up to three years.[16] Once weaned, a diet high in starch and low in protein further exacerbated their nutritional deficiencies. Therefore, both mother and child often lacked sufficient levels of calcium, magnesium, and thiamin crucial to a healthy diet.[17] Those children who did not die of malnourishment or starvation often succumbed to fevers or respiratory infections. Consequently, only half of enslaved children survived past age five.[18]

Despite such high infant and child mortality, a few slave owners placed a value on enslaved children before any abolitionist petitions came before Parliament. John Poole, an attorney for Hope Estate in St. Andrew, was distressed when he learned that the estate discontinued the practice of providing enslaved children with meals in 1774. Although Hope Estate lacked sufficient provisions to continue feeding each child, Poole ordered that the practice be resumed, and even went so far as to make arrangements to purchase the necessary goods in Kingston. "This you are sensible will be a little Expensive," he wrote in a letter to Richard Elletson, owner of the estate, in January 1775, "but I know you had rather allow it than give up a Custom so human and beneficial in all respects."[19] Two years later, Hope Estate discontinued the practice again. This time it was Anna Eliza Elletson, Richard Elletson's widow, who wrote to Poole: "I beg you will order it to be reviv'd, and also that particular care may be taken of the breeding women, and their Children, for you well know, that on the number, and health of the Negroes, Depends the Success of a

Plantation."[20] In 1778, she angrily wrote Poole again, concerned that "the increase of the Negroes, is by no means proportionable to the decrease, I know not how to account for this."[21] Whether or not the meals resumed, we do not know; this second note suggests that they did, but the damage caused by malnutrition was too severe to be reversed.

Other Jamaican planters felt the same way and sent similar instructions to their estate managers. In 1778 Ezekiel Dickenson directed the managers of his estates in St. Elizabeth to give the "Breeding Wenches some additional cloathing for themselves & Children."[22] By 1784 Nathaniel Phillips required all "Negro Children to be thoroughly looked over every Sunday morns. To be kept clear of vermin & worms & Victuals provided for them . . . every day."[23] Most planters and estate managers, however, preferred to make estate improvements instead. Immediately upon his appointment as manager of Dundee Estate in St. Mary, J. Fowler voiced his concern about the condition of the enslaved population and requested the construction of a thirty-thousand-gallon water tank for the slaves and livestock in April 1787. Three months later, he built six new houses in the slave village out of red and white oak staves "of excellent quality [because] the negroe houses are very indifferent." By September 1787, he had reshingled the estate hospital, stating that such improvements, neglected by his predecessor, were necessary for the livelihood of the enslaved population.[24]

Such improvements to Jamaican estates and the enslaved population as a whole were a direct response to the recent intensification of abolitionist sentiment against the Atlantic slave trade, and as a result, Parliament and the Jamaican Assembly began to look more closely at the enslaved population in an effort to ascertain the reasons for their decrease. Although Stephen Fuller, agent for Jamaica, argued that "the natural increase of slaves in Jamaica is prevented by immoderate labour & cruel usage," many also placed the blame on the slave community itself.[25] After a series of investigations, both legislative bodies concluded in 1788 that natural increase was largely impeded by an inequality of the sexes on Jamaican estates, the want of proper child-rearing regulations, the prevalence of disease among infants and children below the age of four, and the frequent practice of abortions and infanticide among enslaved women.[26] Dr. John Quier, a physician in the parishes of St. John, St. Thomas in the Vale, and Clarendon, with five thousand slaves under his care, argued that many infants died from "the known want of cleanliness, arising from the obstinate attachment of Negro women to their own old customs." According to Quier, many slave mothers did not change their child's clothes for the first three days after giving birth. Dr. James Chisholme, a Clarendon physician with four thousand slaves under his care, argued that it was common practice for enslaved women to bind their children with coarse rags that were soaked with urine in a matter of hours. According to Chisholme, the children then sat in these rags until their mothers saw fit to change them. Therefore, it was commonly believed that "the ignorance, obstinacy, and inattention of Negroes" made any progress toward natural increase close to impossible.[27]

Despite such claims, Jamaican physicians offered only marginal medical attention at best to the large numbers of slaves under their care.[28] Like Quier and Chisholme, for instance, Dr. Adam Anderson, a physician in the parish of St. Ann, had over four thousand slaves under his care.[29] Very few estates had doctors or hospitals of their own, and most Jamaican physicians traveled from estate to estate doctoring only when the illness was beyond the capabilities of the overseer or midwife. Other estates went without a midwife or nurse. When a slave woman by the name of Teresa went into labor on Egypt Estate in Westmoreland in June 1752, Thistlewood sent a "Negro and Mule to Salt River to fetch the Midwife."[30] This lack of consideration for the health and well-being of the slaves on their estates shows the disregard Jamaican planters held for the lives of their slaves, slave pregnancy, and the children that resulted. Despite the need for proper medical attention and healthy slaves on their estates, Jamaican planters still preferred to purchase slaves newly imported from Africa.[31]

It goes without saying that slaves largely took care of themselves and their children during this early period. Jamaican assemblymen and planters felt that this gave the slave community a window of opportunity to perform frequent acts of abortion and infanticide. Before abolitionist sentiment began to threaten the slave supply from Africa, planters largely ignored and even condoned such acts. At Egypt Estate, Thistlewood knew of a doctor who gave "the Wild Negroe Women who frequently apply to him, Something which makes them Barren."[32] Planter objections came only when the procedures affected the well-being of their slaves, as was the case with one woman named Grace who died in October 1783 "of a mortification in the womb after an abortion."[33]

Once Jamaican planters realized a need for more children, however, abortion and infanticide suddenly became plagues on the island. Unable to understand or acknowledge the conditions on their estates, most planters justified the high infant and child mortality rates by pointing fingers at the slave community instead of looking in the mirror. However, where planters saw abortions and infanticide, miscarriages and infant mortality were often just as likely to blame. Although it is doubtful that enslaved women performed these acts to the degree Jamaican planters alleged, the women knew that their children had little chance for survival. Some women considered having children a burden, especially with the lack of pre- and postnatal care. Others refused to bring a child into a world of slavery. As a result, some enslaved women performed abortions or arranged for their child's death soon after its birth. Dr. Collins, a Jamaican physician, seemed to understand their situation when he wrote, "Upheld by no consolation, animated by no hope, her nine months of torment issue in the production of a being, doomed, like herself to the rigours of eternal servitude, and aggravating, by its claims on maternal support the weight of her own evils."[34] Acts like these were easy to conceal with such high rates of miscarriage and infant mortality.

The Development of Pro-Natal and Ameliorative Policies in Eighteenth-Century Jamaica

As abolitionist petitions against the slave trade gradually began to gain Parliamentary support in the eighteenth century, Jamaican planters anxiously imagined the possibility of a future without the slave trade. If slave importations suddenly stopped, planters knew, they could not rely on the present condition of the enslaved population. In 1789, Bryan Edwards calculated the annual rate of decrease to be almost 2.5 percent per year, while Robert Hibbert argued in 1790 that it could be as high as 5 percent.[35] "A step of life is wanting on most Estates," Sir William Young said in 1791 at a meeting of Parliament, "leaving a chasm between childhood and mature man."[36] Young's statement shows the changes taking place in English ideas about slavery in the colonies, not only toward natural increase but toward slave childhood as well. As abolitionism gained significant ground in England, Jamaican planters strategically purchased more breeding women, girls, and children from West African ports.[37] While that would serve as a quick fix, they gradually came to the realization that they needed to focus their attention more fully on the slaves already on their estates in order to close that gap between childhood and adulthood and hopefully render future slave importations unnecessary.

In 1788, the Jamaican Assembly passed the first set of laws specifically designed to ameliorate the condition of the slave community and promote the natural increase of the enslaved population.[38] Although these laws did not require plantation owners to lessen the workload of their slaves, these new laws did grant each slave an annual clothing allowance and required planters to provide one acre of land for every ten slaves to be used as provision grounds. Furthermore, estate managers were required to provide each slave with the necessary time to rest and work their provision grounds. In order to ensure this, the Jamaican Assembly subjected each estate manager to a monthly inspection and required a report on the acreage and condition of the slaves' provision grounds, as well as proof that each slave received his or her annual clothing allowances under a penalty of 50 pounds colonial currency. As we saw with Fowler's efforts on Dundee Estate in St. Mary, some had already begun to make minor improvements. The Jamaican Assembly, desperate to increase the island's enslaved population by natural means, used these laws and the ameliorative amendments that followed to force all planters to appreciate the slaves already laboring on their estates and to rely less on the slave trade.[39]

These laws also forced Jamaican planters to reevaluate the nature of childhood on their estates. Overnight, physicians gained more responsibility by becoming the eyes and ears of the Jamaican Assembly. Suddenly each plantation had a physician on site, either daily or weekly, monitoring the health of the enslaved population and the conduct of the estate managers. In order to "more effectually prevent the destruction of Negroes by executive labour and unreasonable punishments," every surgeon, as required by oath and penalty of law, annually reported the increase and decrease of the slaves under their care.[40] At the same time, the Consolidated Slave Law enacted a reward system to provide incentives for natural increase as well as the better treatment of slaves. Each overseer received an award of 20 shillings colonial currency for each child born on the estate and kept alive during the time of the report, and estate owners received a tax deduction equaling the same amount.[41] Again the estate physician had the upper hand, as Jamaican law required proof of birth in the form of a physician's certificate before any reward or tax deduction was granted. Although planters still viewed children as economic liabilities when they were young, this law recognized that the only way to stall abolitionists was to acknowledge that children could grow up to be productive adults.

The Assembly's plans worked, and estate owners and managers began to enact their own reward system to ensure population and economic growth at the plantation level. Many planters gave a dollar to each woman and midwife who successfully birthed a live child "and told them, that for the future they might claim the same sum . . . for every infant which should be brought to the overseer alive and well."[42] Bernard Ezekiel and William Dickenson, owners of several estates in St. Elizabeth, ordered that each mother receive one pound of fresh meat and extra clothing for herself and every child under ten.[43] Lord Penrhyn periodically increased the rewards given to midwives and mothers on his estates, and by 1805 enslaved newborns received "a Fowl to commence its little stock in life."[44] Although these incentives seemed excessive to some planters, others felt that these rewards were merely sound economic investments for the future. Meanwhile, lessening work demands never entered the discussion.

Only in 1801, when the Jamaican Assembly amended the Consolidated Slave Law of 1788 by decreeing that all mothers with six or more living children receive an exemption from all estate labor, were work demands addressed.[45] Yet, this measure only provided an incentive for enslaved women to have more children and to keep alive those children they already had. This latest version of the Consolidated Slave Law, and every version following it, took no measures to reduce the number of hours enslaved men, women, and children worked in the fields or in the trades. Nor did these laws attempt to improve working conditions either. So, while the idea of amelioration gave planters hope for the future, it was just that: an idea. The hard labor and harsh working conditions endemic on Jamaica's estates negated any ameliorative benefits that came to the enslaved population. Planters failed to understand that, without measures in place addressing the nature of work, amelioration was doomed to fail.

As laws like these laid the foundation for what many planters believed would spark a natural increase of the enslaved population, some slaves began to characterize certain enslaved women, especially those exempt from labor, as "belly-women" by the nineteenth century.[46] Although archival sources do not indicate whether the term was a mark of respect or ridicule, labels like these indicate that the slave community came to understand the special significance of "breeding wenches." Matthew "Monk" Lewis argued that his slaves even understood the importance planters placed on natural increase. On his arrival to Cornwall Estate in 1815, he noted several enslaved women who thrust their children in his face and said, "See massa, see! Here nice new neger me bring for work for massa!"[47] Although Lewis believed that these women were trying to impress him with their fertility, their actions also suggest that some enslaved Jamaicans realized that amelioration was motivated more by personal greed than by humanitarianism.

As children became more desirable commodities on Jamaican estates, they became more visible in the estate and plantation inventories. Instead of merely listing the number of slaves, bookkeepers organized them into categories such as first gang, second gang, children's gang, invalids, domestics, and children of nonworking age. By 1796, for example, Braco Estate in St. James devoted an entire page to "children each mother has had and date of their birth."[48] The following year the Jamaican periodical *Columbian Magazine* began reporting instances of great fertility on the island, such as enslaved women who gave birth to triplets or had over nine living children, as if to brag in some sort of macabre show and tell.[49] Therefore, the planters who once discouraged pregnancy and ignored the children on their estates now revealed a sense of pride in the natural increase of their slaves, indicating a significant shift in the perception of childhood.

Some planters tried to create an environment more conducive to natural increase by providing pre- and postnatal care for the enslaved women on their estates. In the hopes that enslaved women would carry their children to term, many planters lightened their workloads during pregnancy. On Halse Hall in Clarendon, for example, owner Henry de la Beche put all pregnant women in the second gang as soon as he learned of their condition. "She is not compelled to do even the light work of that gang," de la Beche wrote in 1825, "the intention being merely to keep her in sight, and prevent her from carrying heavy loads for herself." Planters like de la Beche kept pregnant women in the second and third gang up to the seventh or eighth month of pregnancy, then sent them home until the fourth or sixth week after giving birth. Planters hoped that this time would enable the women to give birth to a healthy child and to have sufficient time to recuperate. They also hoped that the women would use this lying-in period to secure the health of their newborns by giving them extra attention in an environment free from the distractions of field labor.[50]

Jamaican planters also hired new estate managers with such qualities "as that of taking especial care of the negro children."[51] For instance, Charles Gordon Gray replaced his overseer with one "particularly careful in looking after the sick and raising children."[52] Meanwhile, planters and estate mangers continued to improve the medical care of their slaves, often with a direct focus on natural increase. They built hospitals on their estates and began inoculating their slaves in an effort to protect them against smallpox.[53] Lewis built a second hospital on Cornwall Estate in Westmoreland in 1815 for the seriously ill, reserving the first for minor complaints.[54] Planters also consulted the first self-help books of the day, such as *Practical Rules for the Management and Medical Treatment of Negro Slaves, in the Sugar Colonies* and *Practical Remarks on the Management of Breeding Women during Pregnancy, Lying-in, &c* for advice on how best to manage the children and pregnant women on their estates.[55] Suddenly enslaved children who were once financial burdens became crucial components to the survival and protection of Jamaican slavery.

Life on a Jamaican Plantation

Even as planters gradually implemented ameliorative improvements on their estates in an effort to preserve the institution of slavery, enslaved parents and their children went about constructing their own lives as best they could. There is a large historiography on Jamaican slavery, but few scholars have examined enslaved children outside of quantitative studies of infant and child mortality.[56] Therefore, before examining whether these pro-natal policies succeeded in increasing the enslaved population, I will first describe the private lives of enslaved children on Jamaican plantations. Although our knowledge of child development in the slave villages is limited, archival sources do offer glimpses into the experiences of enslaved children on Jamaican estates during this period, experiences defined by instability, immense poverty, overwork, and death.

The majority of Jamaica's enslaved children lived in a complex social environment composed of small groups of people living together in thatched huts of one or two rooms containing sparse furnishings, an iron pot and a few cooking utensils, and a few yabbaware and calabash bowls.[57] While historians such as Barry Higman have argued that slaves largely lived in nuclear families of two parents and their children, Elsa Goveia and others have stressed the presence of matrifocal families composed strictly of a woman and her children.[58] More recently, Trevor Burnard has argued that the presence of matrifocal families has been exaggerated and that slaves tried to reduce the degree of matrifocality that existed within the slave quarters.[59] It appears, then, that although some Jamaican enslaved children did live in nuclear and matrifocal familial units, historians are beginning to suggest a more intricate environment. Therefore, a concentration on nuclear or matrifocal families oversimplifies the complex nature of life in the slave villages.

Evidence suggests that some enslaved children belonged to kin-like groups created long before they were born. "I asked one of my Negro servants this morning whether old Luke was a relation of his," Lewis, the owner of Cornwall Estate in Westmoreland, wrote in 1817. "'Yes,' he said, 'He and my father were shipmates.'"[60] Separated from their natal kinship networks in West Africa either through warfare, famine, or kidnapping, African children and adults found themselves thrust into the horrors of the Middle Passage, slave auctions, and a new life among strangers. In order to survive they developed new strategies of coping by identifying themselves with those who shared similar experiences and re-creating the bonds of kinship in order to find support and strength in the midst of their pain and fear. Robert Renny, a contemporary historian and Jamaican planter, wrote in 1807, "A ship-mate is one of their most endearing appellations; and they who have been wafted across the Atlantic ocean in the same vessel, ever after look on each other as bretheren."[61] As newly defined brothers and sisters, shipmates looked on their children "mutually as their own."[62] The slave community reinforced these bonds by prohibiting sexual relations between those who traveled together on the same ship.[63] While the shared experiences of the slave trade prompted some Africans who made the crossing together to create new kin-like groups in Jamaica, the slave community acknowledged and respected these newly formed bonds as family.

William Sells, a Jamaican physician, purchased two African children, a young boy and girl, to work as house servants in 1808. As they grew older, they became quite close and considered themselves siblings. When Sells decided to sell them, the children made it clear to him that they would not be separated from each other, and he sold the children together to a buyer living in Spanish Town.[64] Therefore, while some children were born into these newly created kin-like networks, other children created these networks themselves. As West Africans young and old struggled to find a place in the slave villages, these newly formed ties provided stability and a new support network for them as well as their children in an otherwise unstable life.

This creation of new familial and kin-like ties was important for the many enslaved children living apart from their natal kinship groups. Those who were either orphaned or recently purchased from West Africa or a nearby estate in Jamaica lived in the slave villages away from the security of their parents and kin in a new environment of strangers. Some found ways of coping by identifying themselves with a new family or kin-like network or by simply trying to coexist in that small thatched hut. In 1816, Lewis noted the attachment sixteen-year-old Prince felt for Philippa, a woman who adopted Prince in his infancy on Cornwall Estate.

During her long stay in the estate's hospital, Prince spent every moment of his free time by her side.[65] Children like Prince who were orphaned or abandoned in their infancy and were too young to remember their mothers most likely attempted to adjust to their new environment with a substitute mother figure. Those who were orphaned at a much older age and remembered their mothers may have created a new kin-like group with the hope of finding security and acceptance.

Lewis does not state whether Philippa responded in kind toward young Prince. For some women adoption may have meant raising a child imposed on them by their owners; other women accepted these children as their own. Dido, a woman belonging to Friendship Estate in Westmoreland, adopted a four-year-old boy named Baleanes, and a slave named Big Nelly had three children of her own but adopted a fourth.[66] Estate managers may have forced Dido and Big Nelly to raise these children until they could support themselves as adults; the sources are not clear. Other instances of motherly affection toward adopted children are easier to discern. When Lewis observed Christian's attentiveness and anxiety about the precarious conditions of her own child as well as that of her adopted infant, who both lay sick in Cornwall Estate's hospital, he noted that "no one would discover which was her own child and which the orphan."[67]

Although many enslaved children lived in houses with natal or adopted kin, a few lived in collective "family villages" in the larger confines of the slave quarters. On Hope Estate in St. Andrew in 1818, for example, enslaved children resided with their natal or adopted kin in household clusters, where whole families resided in separate houses surrounded by a wall or fence with one gate. In the center of this family village sat the house of "the principle among them," which was "very superior to the others."[68] Although it is unknown whether this principal was the matriarch or patriarch of the family or whether the majority of the slaves on Hope Estate during this time were African or Creole, household groupings such as these suggest that some enslaved children lived in enclaves reminiscent of those found in some parts of West Africa. In his archaeological excavations of Montpelier Estate in St. James, Higman uncovered similar household formations, where several houses surrounded a common yard.[69] As Montpelier Estate was largely inhabited by enslaved Creoles in the nineteenth century, this suggests that some West African ideas of family and kinship organization survived, albeit in modified forms.

Despite the presence of extended family and kinship groups, many children faced the trauma of being separated from their family and kinship groups either through death, marronage, or even sale. Rather than perform abortions or acts of infanticide, some women abandoned their children in an effort to escape their lives of servitude. It was not uncommon for bookkeepers to list the names of women who fled the plantation leaving their children behind. Although it is likely that some of these women fully intended to return for their children, many did not. Nanny, a woman hired out to Egypt Estate in Westmoreland by a Mr. Cunningham in 1761, was frequently "wanting" from the estate while her child remained at Egypt.[70] Some women made arrangements for their children, and either took them with them or gave their children to friends who planned to escape. On a plantation in the parish of St. Thomas in the Vale, Roxanna absconded in 1817 with her six children as well as three of Oryanna's and three of Daphne's.[71] It could be that Oryanna and Daphne made arrangements with Roxanna and planned to join her and their children at a later date. Or perhaps they simply wanted their children to be free from slavery. Other women attempted to escape during their pregnancy. On Radnor Plantation in the parish of St. Thomas in the East, three pregnant women attempted to escape in 1822, not long before their due dates.[72] A pregnant Eleanor Davidson escaped with her daughter in 1824, only to be caught and give birth to her son in the Manchester Workhouse that same year.[73]

Other children watched helplessly as they or their parents suddenly found themselves sold to another estate. Although the Jamaican Assembly passed a law in 1735 stipulating that families sold to pay a debt could not be separated, that law made no provision for those families not sold as payment of a debt.[74] When the Duke of Manchester relocated to England in 1827, he manumitted Catherine Gray but sold her two children to a Miss Rennall for 60 pounds colonial currency.[75] The Jamaican Assembly did not add an amendment preventing the separation of families to the Consolidated Slave Laws until 1832, just one year before the Emancipation Act of 1833.[76]

While some children accepted their fate, others refused to be separated from their parents. In August 1781, a boy named John was sold at public auction in Spanish Town. In March 1782, John's new owners listed him as a runaway in the Kingston *Royal Gazette*. Although his exact whereabouts were unknown, his new owners believed that he was "lurking around" Spanish Town in search of his mother, who lived there as a slave. While archival sources do not indicate whether John was captured by the authorities or reunited with his mother, his actions indicate that he refused to accept this forced separation from his mother.[77]

Whether some planters respected the bonds of kinship as best as they knew how or simply did not understand the law, a few did not want to separate children from their families. Benjamin Scott Moncrieffe, a mulatto Jamaican planter and former slave himself, made a habit of purchasing women together with their children.[78] Francis Graham, the manager of Georgia Estate in St. Thomas in the East, had no understanding of the law when he wrote in 1816, "We can only now purchase by families & to get ten able people from 25 to 30 must be purchased."[79] Although Graham seems to speak more out of exasperation than caring understanding, his comments are telling. The Assembly simply did not want to separate families and so created a law prohibiting the practice.

Beginning in 1818, Jamaican law defined a slave family as "a man and his wife, his, her, or their, children," despite the fact that many estate owners rarely knew the father of every child in their possession.[80] This definition, however, failed to recognize the complex familial and kin-like bonds that existed in Jamaica's slave villages. Consequently, unrecognized familial units were separated. In 1821, ten-year-old Henry and his grandmother Betsy Newell were domestic slaves at King's House in Spanish Town. While the records give no indication whether Henry's mother was deceased or living in another location at the time, Henry was sold, while his grandmother remained at King's House.[81] Although we have no idea whether Henry and his grandmother had a close relationship, she could have been the only mother he had ever known. Without warning, Henry found himself separated from her and the stability of his life at King's House. Therefore, while some children were sold with their mothers, other children left behind a father, grandmother, or a support network they themselves defined as family or kin.

Labor expectations and pressures from above further challenged the emotional development of Jamaican enslaved children. From birth, they lived in an environment that constantly reinforced their status as slaves. Before the advent of pro-natal policies, enslaved women returned to work immediately or at most a few days after giving birth, with their children tied to their backs. There the children would stay until old enough to begin working on the estates themselves. With amelioration came the creation of plantation nurseries, where children spent their days away from their mothers in the care of female slaves unable to perform any other productive labor on the estate. Some estates kept their nurseries in the center of the slave village in a thatched hut, with wet nurses on hand to breastfeed the children.[82] On these estates, managers and overseers felt it best to keep children away from the fields and exposure to the elements. Although this kept them out of the fields, children still watched as their mothers left before sunrise and came to collect them after sundown. Other estates preferred to keep the children closer to the fields and their mothers, where the children watched their mothers labor in the sun and suffer under the whip.

Children stayed in the plantation nurseries for an average of five years, after which they were branded with the estate's symbol and put under the care of another elderly woman who supervised their introduction into plantation labor.[83] It was at this young age that children in the small gang, sometimes called the children's gang, performed menial tasks "merely to preserve them from habits of idleness."[84] Working the same twelve-hour days as the adults, they were anything but idle as they weeded and cleaned cane and coffee pieces, collected food for livestock, carried trash, and fertilized crops. Many felt that children were better suited to weed and pick grass, and they were issued small, child-size hoes specifically for that purpose; others were given small baskets to carry manure and trash.[85] Although planters placed these children in the small gang to acclimate them to plantation labor, some performed the same labor as the adults. Each June on Braco Estate in St. James, enslaved children in the small gang planted cane alongside the first gang.[86] On Green Park Estate in Trelawny, children carried cane and dug cane roots just like everyone else.[87] "By this," Thomas Roughly, a Jamaican planter, wrote, "they will be taught to observe the mode of planting and putting the cane in the ground."[88] This also began the socialization process of enslavement, cementing their identity as chattel firmly in their young minds.

Their acculturation to the labors of slavery continued as they moved out of the children's gang and into the second gang as early as age nine or ten. Just as the small gang introduced them to plantation labor, the second gang prepared them for more strenuous labor in the fields. Comprising mainly children between the ages of nine and fifteen, the second gang usually performed the same tasks as the adults.[89] J. Fowler, manager of Dundee Estate in St. Mary, wrote to James Stothert in 1789, "I have now Eighteen able Young people Cutting Canes, I Assure you to my own predjudice, as my Cotton Crop at Thatch Hill is losing for want of picking."[90] Therefore, as Fowler suggests, enslaved children joined the jobbing gangs at this young age as well. Most children continued working in the second gang until they were fifteen or sixteen.

It was during their time in the second gang that girlhood began to suffer more than childhood. Just like the boys who worked alongside them, girls could never escape their identity as slaves. As we have seen, this was impressed upon them from the moment of their birth, and they had been working on the estate as slaves for an average of five years. It was at this age, however, that Jamaica's young female slaves encountered new definitions of childhood and girlhood. Under slavery, the various stages of slave childhood revolved around plantation labor and economic need. Infants and children did not work on the estate, while boys and girls labored in the third and second gangs. Before abolitionist threats to the slave trade and, later, to slavery, boyhood and girlhood began around age five, only to end within ten years as entrance into the first gang signified the beginning of their adulthood.

With increased abolitionist threats to the slave supply and the resulting pressures for slaves to naturally reproduce, Jamaican planters and estate managers added new stages to slave childhood. Labels like *man-boy* and *woman-girl* began to appear in the estate inventories as new categorizations of fourteen- and fifteen-year-olds just on the cusp of puberty. Young girls between fourteen and fifteen, sometimes even as young as twelve or thirteen, were added to the lists of breeding wenches and belly-women. Some planters referred to girls as young as thirteen as *woman-girls*. While this solved planters' problem of having too few breeding wenches on their estates, the new classifications chipped away at an already short girlhood.

These shifting definitions of childhood were subjective as well. Some planters categorized enslaved children between five and eight working in the third gang as *boys* and *girls* but classified the gang in which they worked as the *children's gang*. Interestingly, those same planters categorized all enslaved children not working on the estate as *children*. Other planters classified all enslaved children not working on the estate as *infants*, while the *children* worked in the children's or third gang and the *boys* and *girls* on the estate worked in the second gang.

It was also during this time that a select few of the children moved out of the second gang and into an apprenticeship of sorts that prepared them for an adult life as a domestic slave or tradesman. For children living in urban areas, this apprenticeship period came much earlier, and they began working in the house as soon as possible. Most enslaved children living in the rural areas remained in the fields. As we shall see in chapter 3, many of these apprenticeships were reserved for enslaved children of color, or children legally classified as mulattos by the state.[91] Richard S. Dunn gives some insight into the rarity of such opportunities through his work on Mesopotamia Estate in Westmoreland. According to Dunn, one in two boys remained field hands, while five in six girls stayed in the fields.[92] Although these are estimates for only one estate, they are indicative of the nature of child labor throughout the colony. Verene Shepherd has argued that as few as 10 percent of the enslaved population worked as domestics. She adds further insight in her linkage of labor to racist stereotypes. According to Shepherd, enslaved domestics were usually female, Jamaican-born, and mulatto, not only because they were phenotypically closer to whites but also because they were considered too delicate for field labor.[93] While domestic service for mulatto children was not guaranteed, it was more likely that they would be removed from the second gang if an opening in domestic service became available.

As domestic servants, children between nine and fifteen assisted in food preparation and cooking, cleaned pots and kitchen utensils, and attended their master's or mistress's every whim. In 1752 Thistlewood sent an "African girl child" named Accabbah to Salt River Estate to learn to sew. Ten years later, he apprenticed a nine- or ten-year-old Congolese girl named Sally to Doll, his master seamstress: "She is to work for doll whilst learning, and am to give doll a doubloon when learnt."[94] Others, mostly boys, left the second gang to watch livestock, apprentice under carpenters and artisans, and learn the ways of the boiling houses.

While some children left the second gang for domestic or skilled labor, others became gifts, such as a "young Creolian" who was given to a woman "as her future waiting-maid."[95] In his last will and testament executed in December 1758, Thomas Pinnock of Kingston bequeathed to his five daughters "one negro boy and two negro girls each, to be bought out of Guinea vessels."[96] Although they were given as domestic servants, these children were not treated well by the white children of the planters. Some contemporaries describe the white children as being miniature tyrants, allowed to kick and strike their slaves at their discretion. John Riland, a Jamaican planter, remembered that his own parents "allowed me to insult, strike, and kick them as I pleased."[97] Another Jamaican planter, John Stewart, wrote in 1823 that "such ideas [are] gradually nurtured" by the planters, adding, "Should the little black retaliate the ill usage she meets, she is immediately chastised for her impertinence."[98] While domestic enslaved children may have been given a higher status than those children toiling in the fields, they were constantly reminded that they were merely property, even by white children their own age.

Most enslaved children played a part in the growth of their household economy whenever possible. In 1767 Thistlewood noted that Little Member's children on Egypt Estate frequently sold ducks, for example.[99]

Children five years and older also assisted their households in tending the provision grounds and often accompanied enslaved women to the Sunday markets to sell their harvest.[100] Other children resorted to stealing in an effort to find food. In April 1789, a boy named Drake appeared before the St. Ann Slave Court for stealing a steer "with Force and Arms" from Joseph Price with another slave named Quashy.[101] Thistlewood frequently noted instances when children stole food and sugar cane, either to consume or to sell in the Savanna-La-Mar market.[102] Although most Jamaican plantations periodically increased the acreage of their provision grounds in an ameliorative effort to provide their slaves with more food, children continued to sell or steal in order to survive.

One can only surmise how children's experiences as slaves shaped or obstructed their psychological development, but archival sources do suggest that children acted out their frustrations in many ways. Some turned to crime as an outlet. There are frequent reports of children appearing before the island's slave courts for committing acts of theft, violence, vandalism, arson, disturbing the peace, or for directing "Violent and Indecent language in the Public Street" toward free and white residents.[103] While the courts defined these acts as 'crimes, it is just as likely that they were acts of resistance from the perspective of the children themselves. Some children appeared before the slave courts for more serious crimes, indicating that they were capable of resisting their situation as strongly as adults. According to Lewis, one fifteen-year-old girl named Minetta appeared before the Westmoreland Slave Court sometime between 1815 and 1817 for attempting to poison her owner.[104]

Those who did not resist through violence tried to escape in a variety of ways. Some children resorted to alcohol as an escape, a habit that many planters believed they were encouraged to adopt at an extremely young age by their parents.[105] Thistlewood wrote that a boy named Jimmy "was very drunk, with Rum he Stole out of the Bottle."[106] Another of Thistlewood's slaves, Sally, the young Congolese girl apprenticed to Doll, began running away on a regular basis beginning at the age of nine or ten.[107] Rural children were not the only ones to run away, as was the case with a fourteen-year-old boy named Hope who escaped from his Kingston owner William Hawkins in December 1779.[108] Although most Jamaican enslaved children progressed through their childhood without any chance of freedom, instances like these suggest that some refused to accept their position despite their young age.

Truth or Consequences: The Effects of Jamaica's Pro-Natal and Ameliorative Policies

Although child resistance concerned slave owners, ultimately their main goal was to increase the number of enslaved children on their estates. With this interest came a great deal of pressure from all parties involved. While pushing Parliament for strengthened ameliorative legislation, colonists also pressured the Jamaican Assembly to improve the condition of the slaves "so as to render future importations unnecessary."[109] As Jamaican law gradually intensified the rewards and incentives paid for natural increase, pregnancy and childhood rose in value and worth in the minds of the planters as well as the assemblymen. Even though enslaved children were now valuable investments, their numbers still were not as high as many planters would have liked.

Frustrated by the enslaved population's inability to increase naturally, the Jamaican Assembly succumbed to parliamentary and local pressure and adopted the Registration Bill in 1816, which required each slave owner to register his slaves with the colony and Parliament every three years. English humanitarians fighting the international slave trade and subsequent illegal imports into the English colonies first passed the bill in 1810. The English Crown Colony of Trinidad was the first to adopt the bill, in 1812, and other British West Indian colonies soon followed. By 1815, weary of abolitionist attacks and charges of cruelty and oppression, the Jamaican Assembly entertained the bill "because the slaves have not increased, but diminished, in number, and a different and natural order of things is not likely to take place." Subsequently, beginning in 1817, the Assembly required triennial returns from each slaveholder listing name, sex, age, color, country of origin, and any additional remarks, usually the mother's name if known. By 1820, the returns included the increase and decrease of the enslaved population, specifically noting whether these changes resulted from births, deaths, sales, gifts, manumissions, transportations, or desertions.[110]

Although the Registry Bill was originally designed to curtail illicit slave imports, the Jamaican Assembly used the triennial returns to chart the increase and decrease of slaves on the island and to apply more pressure on planters to further ameliorate their slaves. As we have already seen, the Consolidated Slave Laws required each planter to inspect provision grounds, to submit proof that their slaves received their annual clothing allowances, and to provide an annual summary of the increase and decrease of slaves on their estates with a specified cause of death. Despite the threat of penalties and fines, most parish vestries failed to enforce the laws. The Registry Bill added more pressure by attaching the weight of a parliamentary decree and placing a £100 penalty on every missing name.[111]

Planters typically transferred much of the legislative pressure to the slaves themselves. As in the past, most planters looked no farther than the mothers for their failure to uphold the owners' expectations. Although planters continued to argue that women performed abortions and acts of infanticide, they frequently complained that their women bred too slowly. "It is just as hens will frequently not lay eggs on shipboard," Lewis wrote, "because they do not like their situation." In a March 1817 journal entry, Lewis expressed his anger at one woman who miscarried in her eighth month of pregnancy. He complained that despite giving her ample food and clothing, her situation was becoming habitual. He further lamented that out of the 150 females on Cornwall Estate, there were only eight listed on the breeding list for that year. "How they manage it so ill I know not," he wrote, "but somehow or other certainly the children do not come."[112]

Other planters extended the blame to the midwives on their estates. In April 1830, for example, the manager of Rose Hall Estate in St. James blamed a midwife named Dorinda for all child deaths that took place that year. He sent her to the fields as punishment "for general neglect in the performance of her duty that is proper to." That day she ran away, only to return the following evening. A few months later, the daughter of a slave woman named Elizabeth Palmer died a few days after her birth "from neglect of Dorinda the midwife, being the fourth child in succession by her." What happened to Dorinda after this incident is unknown, but the estate manager believed that she, not the conditions on the estate, was the ultimate cause of Rose Hall's failure to increase naturally that year.[113]

Although Jamaican plantations and estates experienced fluctuations in natural increase throughout this period, the enslaved population as a whole continued to decrease naturally. As can be seen in Table 1, very few parishes exhibited a natural increase in their enslaved population; and between 1817 and 1832, the enslaved population as a whole gradually decreased with each triennial return. While eleven of the twenty-one parishes showed a positive natural increase between 1817 and 1820, these rates fluctuated throughout the remaining years of slavery. Seven of the twenty-one parishes failed to increase their enslaved population during

TABLE 1. RATE OF NATURAL INCREASE, 1817–1832

	Natural increase per 1,000 per annum				
Parish	1817–20	1820–23	1823–26	1826–29	1829–32
Westmoreland	-7.4	-8.1	-5.1	-5.1	-5.2
Hanover	-5.9	-5.3	-6.2	-8.3	-8.4
St. James	-3.1	-7.7	-7.5	-5.4	-8.6
Trelawny	-1.0	-5.4	-5.2	-6.8	-6.6
St. Elizabeth	+5.8	+4.5	+5.0	+9.0	+7.4
Manchester	+5.1	+4.2	+6.0	+7.4	+6.4
St. Ann	+1.8	-0.6	+1.6	+2.6	+3.9
Clarendon	+1.2	-6.9	-2.4	-0.3	-7.1
Vere	-2.3	-1.9	+2.3	-0.7	+1.1
St. Dorothy	-2.8	-4.4	-3.3	+3.2	-6.6
St. Thomas in the Vale	+2.1	-0.5	-4.2	-3.3	-9.6
St. John	+3.1	-5.5	-1.5	-5.3	-9.1
St. Catherine	+2.4	-0.4	+1.5	+6.2	-2.4
St. Mary	-6.1	-5.0	-6.9	-10.2	-12.8
St. Andrew	+3.6	+3.6	+4.0	-2.1	-4.6
Port Royal	+10.9	+4.8	+5.4	+4.8	+2.1
St. David	+2.9	-3.8	-4.9	-6.1	-4.1
St. George	-1.1	-3.7	-2.7	-15.6	-7.9
Portland	-2.5	+1.4	-2.9	-7.2	-4.7
St. Thomas in the East	-5.7	-8.6	-4.9	-12.0	-10.5
Kingston	*+3.0*	*+2.0*	*+0.2*	*+1.3*	*-1.8*
Total	-0.7	-3.1	-2.1	-3.4	-4.8

Source: Higman, *Slave Population and Economy*, 102.

even one of the six trienniums. St. Ann was the only parish to improve over this fifteen-year period; the three parishes of St. Elizabeth, Manchester, and Port Royal were the only parishes to exhibit a positive natural increase for the entire period. Port Royal's natural increase, however, actually declined between 1817 and 1832 from +10.9 to +2.1. If slavery had not been abolished in 1834, it is quite possible that the parish would have shown a decrease in population by the next triennial return.

Although we know that the enslaved population failed to naturally increase during this period, we may never truly know how amelioration affected infant and child mortality on the island. Ameliorative efforts on estates such as Maryland Estate in St. Andrew improved infant mortality, yet child mortality still remained high. All of the twenty children who died on Maryland Estate between 1817 and 1825 were above the age of five; amelioration clearly did not protect enslaved children from the horrors of plantation labor.[114] Of the thirty-five slaves who died between 1822 and 1825 on Radnor Plantation in St. Thomas in the East, twenty-six were children.[115] Only four, however, were infants and children under four. This suggests that ameliorative efforts improved the quality of life for slave infants, while little changed for enslaved children. Once they left the nursery and began working in the children's gang, their malnourished bodies succumbed to exhaustion, hard labor, and harsh treatment.

It is possible that Jamaican plantations and estates underrecorded the infant mortality in their slave villages; as a result the number of children who died in the days and weeks after their birth would not appear in plantation and estate accounts or the triennial returns. This is a theory held by George Roberts, who argues that any child who was born and died in that three-year period between returns was never recorded.[116] If this is true, although more children survived into adolescence, it is quite possible that a large percentage of children continued to die in the first weeks of life unbeknownst to the Jamaican Assembly and Parliament. However, given the obsession of planters regarding the state of natural decrease on the island and its relation to their profit margins, that is unlikely. Barry Higman is probably right in his assumption that the degree of underrepresentation was no more than 1 percent of the total enslaved population.[117]

Archival sources also suggest that amelioration had little effect on slave fertility. Between 1817 and 1832, despite the presence of rewards and other incentives, birth rates throughout the island declined. Planters registered 24,346 births in 1820 but only 22,138 in 1832.[118] Although women received marginal maternity leave before and after giving birth, backbreaking labor, harsh treatment, and a vitamin-deficient diet still worked against their bodies. The strain of frequent pregnancies, miscarriages, and childbirth also took a toll on their health and reproductive systems. The population would not begin to increase naturally until the postemancipation period for precisely these reasons.

Summary

Throughout this period of amelioration, Jamaican planters continued to see nothing other than their own goals for profit and increase. Even during the last years of slavery, planters failed to realize that the natural decrease of the enslaved population could be attributed to anything other than their condition as slaves. Although amelioration provided additional food, clothing, and medical care, it was not enough; the enslaved population continued to decrease as fertility declined. Although more infants survived, child mortality plagued slave villages. Therefore, the quality of life for Jamaica's enslaved children failed to change under amelioration. Despite the fact that infants received better care and attention, their shift from the nursery to the children's gang was a hard one that took a devastating toll on their bodies and psyches.

As the nature of slavery changed on the island, these changes motivated shifts in planter opinions of child worth. In 1788, planters began to see children more as investments than burdens. Although planters' ideas of child worth changed, their ideas of childhood as they related to the enslaved population really had not. It is true that Jamaican planters no longer ignored the children on their estates and took steps to improve their way of life; these initiatives, however, were motivated more by a desire for economic gain than humanitarianism. Most planters still failed to see them as children. Instead enslaved children were merely investments and a means of protecting West Indian interests in Parliament.

As Jamaican planters used enslaved children to lead them toward the economic stability and profitability they craved, the children continued their struggle for survival. We will never know the extent of how their experiences as slaves damaged their psychological and emotional development; we can only imagine how a life filled with death, disease, and harsh labor affected them. As these children left the plantation nurseries for the fields, they rapidly shifted from child to adult. Forced to grow up at an extremely early age, they would never escape the traumas they faced on a daily basis despite their acts of resistance and violence. As planters increasingly acknowledged that children could grow up to be productive adults, boys quickly matured into laborers and tradesmen and girls became breeding wenches and belly-women. Destined for bigger things on the estate, their short childhood ended almost as soon as it began. As we will see, the psychological damages of slavery stretched even to enslaved children with white fathers, who found themselves marginalized by their dual identity but elevated in the Jamaican plantation complex by their whiteness.

2 / "The child whom many fathers share, Hath seldom known a father's care": Miscegenation and Childhood in Jamaican Slave Society

In 1764, an unnamed slave woman belonging to the Clarendon parish rectory gave birth to a daughter she named and baptized Molly Matthews. According to parish rectors, Molly was the reputed daughter of a white man named David Matthews. Four years later, David Matthews applied for Molly's manumission and provided a new slave woman in exchange for her freedom. Unfortunately for Matthews and his daughter, the parish rector stole Molly's replacement and left the parish before her manumission paperwork could be processed. The two were never seen again, and the Clarendon Vestry rescinded the order until Matthews provided a new slave. Matthews never supplied the parish rectory with another enslaved woman, so Molly remained enslaved herself. Thirty years later, in November 1794, a more sympathetic Clarendon Vestry championed Molly's case and petitioned the Jamaican Assembly for her freedom. This time, with little debate, the Assembly manumitted Molly and her four children. Interestingly, the Assembly did not require the customary replacement slaves for Molly or her children, and the thirty-year-old mother walked out of the Clarendon rectory with her family to begin her life as a free woman.[1]

While Molly's manumission experience is unique, her life experiences are exemplary of what many children in her situation faced in Jamaica during this period. Her status as a mulatto, the child of an enslaved woman and a white man, set her apart from the rest of the slave community. In addition to having manumission opportunities that most enslaved children only dreamed of, some slaves like Molly enjoyed certain benefits from being a child of mixed parentage. Although her father attempted to secure her freedom while she was a child, her experiences with the manumission process illustrate the difficulties and setbacks that many people of color faced while trying to attain their freedom. While Molly was lucky to gain the support of the Clarendon Vestry in her adulthood, many progressed through their childhood without even a sliver of hope for freedom.

This chapter places Molly and her peers in the context of the slave experience in Jamaica. After examining concubinage and miscegenation on the island, I will discuss the social stratification of the children who resulted from such unions. In order to understand the place of mulatto children in Jamaican slave society and their relationship to the changing nature of childhood, I will delve deeper into their experiences as slaves in order to explore how that social stratification sometimes allowed them to receive better positions on Jamaican plantations but devalued their worth as slaves. Finally, I will question the relationship these children had with their white fathers in terms of inheritance, manumission, and acceptance. Despite their limited worth to Jamaican planters, the existence of enslaved children of color complicated planter ideas of childhood by forcing many members of white society to acknowledge and gradually accept their identity as children apart from their status as slaves.

Concubinage, Miscegenation, and Status in Jamaican Slave Society

Throughout this period, Jamaican society was highly stratified and color largely defined social status. The historian and planter Edward Long described Jamaican society as being divided into "three ranks of men (white, mulatto, and black) dependent on each other, and rising in a proper climax of subordination, in which the whites would have the highest place."[2] Although population estimates vary for this period, the contemporary historian Bryan Edwards estimates that around thirty thousand whites, ten thousand free black and free people of color, and 250,000 enslaved men, women, and children lived on the island at the end of the eighteenth century.[3] Resembling a social pyramid, these three ranks contained various subcategories that were arranged by myriad qualifiers and were defined almost exclusively by the white community. Naturally the white community, which constituted the smallest portion of the pyramid, sat at the top. Members of the Jamaican Assembly and absentee planters enjoyed the highest social standing. Jamaican planters and estate owners who resided on the island followed, although most hoped to better their social status by filling future seats in the Assembly or by boosting productivity and profit enough to return to England as an absentee. Merchants and shopkeepers, tradesmen and craftsmen, sailors and members of the military, and estate management sat on the last rung of the white social ladder, consoled only by the knowledge that social advancement was always a possibility.

Free blacks and free people of color, as they were termed by the white community, who were either born free or enslaved, fell below the white community in the social hierarchy of the island. Free people of color, termed *mulattos* by Jamaican law, were the highest members of this social rank but not without social divisions of their own based on skin color, phenotypic attributes, and status at birth. While freeborn children of color benefited from a higher social status than those who were slave-born, mulatto children with the lightest skin and "whose complexion was [not] a prima facie evidence of slavery" were ranked superior in the eyes of Jamaican white society.[4] In his 1793 *History of Jamaica,* Edwards wrote that many took offense when called "by a degree lower than they are."[5] Free blacks followed closely behind the mulatto community, still elevated socially by their freedom but ranked inferior to Jamaican mulattos by both the white and the mulatto community. Although those in the free black community who were born free saw themselves as being socially superior over those who were born slaves, their blackness still linked them to the system of slavery and the stereotypical savagery and ignorance that many in Jamaica attached to those of African descent. In other words, blackness had become synonymous with slavery. Those with darker skin were perceived to be closer to their African past and were categorized accordingly.

The Jamaican enslaved population, ranked below them all, sat at the very bottom of this social pyramid. Ten percent of the enslaved population was classified as mulatto; as a result, the slave community itself was not devoid of social divisions.[6] According to Orlando Patterson, about 63 percent of the enslaved population was Jamaican-born and looked on their African-born counterparts with contempt.[7] Degrees of whiteness, birth, and occupation relegated members of this community to their respective rungs of the social ladder as well. While Jamaican planters placed Creole enslaved children in a moderately higher social standing above those born in Africa, children who worked as domestics or apprentices received more allowances and provisions than the children who labored in the fields. Only about 15 percent of the enslaved population in Jamaica at the turn of the century were domestics or skilled laborers.[8] Mulatto children, however, often filled the most coveted positions on Jamaica's plantations and estates. In fact, many planters and estate managers reserved these positions exclusively for enslaved mulattos.

In his discussion of social stratification, the sociologist Pierre van der Berghe asserts that it is necessary for those in power to maintain their distance from those they deem inferior as a means of maintaining their authority and control. The social stratification that results creates racial stratification, and the community is divided into a caste-like system.[9] In Jamaica, color largely became representative of social status, especially as the "colored" population increased in number. While occupation and *creolité*, or being Jamaican-born rather than African-born, defined social status, the white community placed the most emphasis on color and degrees of whiteness.

Despite the possibility of social mobility, there existed a glass ceiling of sorts between certain rungs of the social ladder. As the Jamaican Assembly enacted codes to keep the enslaved population under control and subordinate, oppressive legislative measures kept free blacks and free people of color at bay. "In fact, the tendency of the colonial laws . . . was to degrade the brown man in his own estimation, to debase him in the eyes of the white community."[10] When free blacks and free children of color became adults, they were not allowed to vote, give evidence against whites in court proceedings, or hold political office. They were relegated to pews at the back of the church, and cemeteries were segregated.[11] Laws were also in place to restrict the amount of money and property free people of color could inherit from their family and the white community, as well as their ability to testify at a trial of their peers.[12] Although the law required free blacks and free men of color to serve in the local militia, they could never rise above the rank of sergeant, and black and colored militiamen were excluded from joining the island's prestigious cavalry regiments.[13] Beginning in 1761, Jamaican law required all free blacks and free people of color regardless of age to carry a certificate of freedom at all times and to wear a blue cross on their right shoulder indicating their status as freedmen under threat of imprisonment. Although Jamaican authorities seldom enforced this law, most in the mulatto community considered the badge to be a mark of disgrace rather than a sign of freedom.[14]

As the white community carefully worked to distance itself from both the free and the enslaved populations, the absence of white women on the island drew many men from the white community to the slave villages and urban slave quarters for companionship. As Catherine Hall notes, except for the wives and daughters who accompanied colonial officials, army and naval officers, clergymen, and missionaries, white women rarely came to the island: "England was for families, Jamaica was for sex."[15] White men notoriously used enslaved women and girls as sexual objects. John Williamson, a plantation doctor in Jamaica, wrote in 1817, "Black and brown mistresses are considered necessary appendages to every establishment. Even a young bookkeeper coming from Europe, is generally instructed to provide himself; and however repugnant may seem the idea at first, his scruples are overcome and he conforms to the general custom."[16] James Mursell Phillippo, a Baptist missionary and eight-year resident of Jamaica, argued that nearly nine-tenths of the male population and even the "lowest white servant had [a] native female companion."[17] What resulted was a form of institutionalized concubinage that became widely accepted and sometimes encouraged in Jamaica, and the British West Indies as a whole, by the nineteenth century.

It is important to note, however, that not every "concubine" granted her consent, nor was she always an adult. Undoubtedly Thomas Thistlewood was one such predator. Throughout the pages of his diaries, the overseer and slave owner detailed his numerous unions with various women of Egypt Estate in Westmoreland. Day or night he took women when and where he pleased, giving most of them two or four bits for their cooperation.[18] In 1751, for example, Thistlewood had frequent sexual liaisons with at least twelve of the twenty-six women and six of the nine girls belonging to the estate.[19] Trevor Burnard discusses Thistlewood's sex life during the thirty-seven years that he lived in Jamaica in fascinating quantitative detail, and one cannot help but formulate the image of a vile and highly sexed predator who had unlimited access to a pool of women and girls who were often powerless to defend themselves from his advances.[20]

Men like Thistlewood certainly felt it was their right to take these women and girls and do with them as they wished. They also allowed outside access to their female slaves, while saving their favorites for themselves. J. B. Moreton, a Clarendon bookkeeper, wrote that some owners and estate managers provided female slaves for friends and visitors to their estates in "a pimp-like action."[21] For some planters, their actions were an exercise in control and submission, while others like Thistlewood felt a sense of entitlement and thought only of themselves and their needs. Husbands, fathers, and children in the slave community were powerless to prevent it, "for a man might know of his wife having laid with the overseer or book-keeper, he dared not resent it, neither to his wife nor to the said overseer or book-keeper," for fear of flogging.[22]

It is important to stress that not all of these liaisons took place between enslaved women and white men, nor were enslaved women the primary targets. Jamaican planters, estate managers, bookkeepers, and overseers also visited young girls in the slave villages and fields. In fact, Burnard suggests that girls working as domestics were far more vulnerable to the sexual advances of Jamaica's planters than those laboring in the fields.[23] The hypersexual Thistlewood is a case in point. As time passed, however, sexual predation became considered inappropriate, indicating further shifts in the definitions of childhood and girlhood as well. In 1816, the Jamaican Assembly attempted to protect enslaved girls under the age of ten from white men by enacting a law stipulating that any carnal knowledge of a female slave below that age was punishable by death.[24] This suggests that the rape of enslaved girls under the age of ten was so prevalent that the Assembly enacted a law to prohibit it; it is also another indication that there was no consideration of childhood or girlhood on Jamaica's estates before the creation of this law. Only when the Assembly passed a law prohibiting this behavior was childhood recognized among the island's slaves. This law defined children as those under ten, whether or not they worked on the estate, suggesting that girlhood began at age ten. Add the labor divisions outlined in chapter 1, and you have girlhood and boyhood ending sometime between the ages of ten and fifteen. It was under these additional circumstances that girls began to suffer sexual predation more than children. Already being reclassified as women-girls and added to the lists of breeding wenches and belly-women, many enslaved girls were unable to protect themselves from the sexual advances of the white men on their estates.

This law was not always enforced or upheld. While working as an overseer of a jobbing gang at Harmony Hall Estate in the parish of St. Thomas in the Vale sometime in the early 1820s, Benjamin M'Mahon realized the appetite of the gang's owner, Adam Steele, for young girls. According to M'Mahon, "Females at the age of ten and eleven fell victims to his brutal lust."[25] M'Mahon does not state whether any of these girls pressed charges against Steele, or if they even knew the nature of the law against such acts. When Kingston authorities charged a white man with chaining down a nine-year-old girl and raping her in 1820, he argued that the girl was chattel and had no rights. Since she could not testify against him, Kingston courts transferred the case to English judges, who ruled in favor of the man.[26] Therefore, although Jamaican law attempted to recognize the delicacy of youth, English law still maintained that slaves were chattel, no matter their age.

In the midst of such indifference to age and consent, some whites took enslaved women and girls as their mistresses. Lady Maria Nugent, wife of Governor George Nugent (1801–5), described how "white men of all descriptions, married or single, live in a state of licentiousness with their female slaves."[27] By entering into a sexual relationship with someone of higher status, enslaved women and girls could reap extra rewards, clothing, and provisions that benefited everyone in their household. Some enjoyed even greater rewards. While he was overseer of Vineyard Pen in St. Elizabeth, Thistlewood built a new house in 1751 for his Congo mistress, Marina. As a housewarming gift, he gave her some sugar, four bottles of rum, some beef, and ten pints of corn made into a medicinal agent called *funje* so that she may treat members of the slave community, "Especially her Ship Mates."[28] Thistlewood not only favored Marina enough to give her a house of her own, but his gift of *funje* suggests that he appreciated her position on the estate as a healer. Furthermore, by noting that the *funje* was a special gift for her shipmates, he inadvertently acknowledged her extended family unit or kinship group as well.

Other slave mistresses received less extravagant gifts than Marina. Some were given colorful beads or a little extra cloth from time to time. William Crookshanks, a bookkeeper and friend of Thistlewood's, often excused his mistress Myrtilla from field labor.[29] With the possibility of such benefits and rewards in the future, becoming the mistress of a white man was a goal that some enslaved women and girls hoped to achieve. According to the Jamaican proprietor Matthew "Monk" Lewis, a slave woman named Psyche on Cornwall Estate in Westmoreland left her husband Nicholas for one of the estate's bookkeepers "because he had a good salary, and could afford to give her more presents than a slave could."[30] Accepting the role of slave mistress or concubine, whether happily or through gritted teeth, not only benefited but improved one's health and well-being.[31]

When these relationships resulted in children, the benefits and rewards could increase. Phibbah, who was Thistlewood's mistress for thirty-three years while he was overseer at Egypt Estate, bore him at least one child. She received a pony and a Nago enslaved girl of her own named Bess in 1765, five years after the birth of their son John.[32] Interestingly, this gift of an eleven-year-old enslaved girl came not from Thistlewood but from John's teacher, Mrs. Sarah Bennett.[33] Clearly some in the white community understood and acknowledged the position of slave mistresses in the plantation complex; such a gift signified acceptance of, even respect for Phibbah's place by Thistlewood's side. In addition to giving Phibbah larger gifts of food, clothing, and jewelry after the birth of his son, Thistlewood allowed her to have frequent overnight visits from her daughter Coobah, a twenty-year-old slave living on nearby Paradise Pen.[34] In fact, according to Burnard, Thistlewood came to see Coobah, later baptized Jenny Young, as his own daughter and often gave her special treatment.[35]

Without children, someone like Phibbah may have been no more than a favorite paramour. With children, women like Phibbah could rise even higher in the social ranks of the slave community to receive property and certain freedoms denied other slaves. Lady Maria Nugent recalled one slave woman on Hope Estate in St. Andrew, "the overseer's chere amie . . . [who] shewed me her three yellow children, and said with some ostentation, she should have another."[36] Lady Nugent's disdain indicates that relationships between white men and enslaved women actually reduced the social status of slave mistresses in the eyes of some white women of the island, yet the woman's eagerness to have another child with Hope Estate's overseer suggests that some enslaved women understood the importance children played in the inner workings of Jamaica's social hierarchy. It is reasonable to assume that this slave woman enjoyed an economic and social status like that of Phibbah on Egypt Estate.

Lady Nugent was not alone in her disapproval of such "licentious" relationships. While some white women, like John Thistlewood's teacher Sarah Bennett, accepted the presence of slave mistresses, others branded these liaisons, and the children who resulted from them, as immoral and unacceptable. Aside from the impropriety of entering into a sexual relationship with someone of much lower social status, the fact that a white man chose someone regarded as savage and of debased moral character was inconceivable to white women. For a husband to take what his wife considered to be a piece of chattel as a mistress was unspeakable. No woman of stature would admit it to her friends and family, let alone to herself. Furthermore, some white women envisioned enslaved women as serpents who used their feminine wiles to ensnare and manipulate white men.[37]

White women were not the only ones who felt this way. One visitor to Kingston in the first decade of the nineteenth century described a city of excess that "creates disgust rather than merits esteem."[38] Many whites believed that living so far from England created an environment that allowed even the most moral Englishman to act as he wished without consequence. The missionary William Knibb wrote to his brother shortly after his arrival to Jamaica in the 1820s, "Let it not be thought that the slave is the only one who is vile. The white population is worse, far worse, than the victims of their injustice."[39]

It is obvious why missionaries and white women disliked fraternization with the enslaved population. Some Jamaican planters also voiced their disapproval and occasionally discouraged their overseers and bookkeepers from entering into relationships with enslaved women on their estates. The planter George Turner conceded that he should not condemn his peers "for those faults we are guilty of ourselves," and he congratulated his estate manager in September 1791 for his "firm perseverance against those attachments that prove so banefull." One month later, however, after learning of another employee's extravagance with a few of the estate's female slaves, Turner threatened that employee with dismissal unless he began to "conduct himself with propriety."[40] Although visits to the slave villages were acceptable to Turner, a relationship that took an administrator's attention away from the everyday business of the estate was not. As we have already seen, many in the white community believed that the influence slave mistresses held over their white lovers challenged the men's position of authority on the estate. The children that resulted from these relationships added even more challenges for the white community by complicating their notions of childhood and slavery.

Life and Labor on Jamaica's Plantations

Only one thing remained secure throughout this entire process of miscegenation: those children born to a slave woman, no matter the status of their father, were slaves themselves. That status came not from the "sins of the fathers, but the misfortunes of the mothers on the children unto the third and fourth generation."[41] As the number of mulatto children grew in the slave villages, so did the social stratification of the enslaved population. Table 2 delineates the various labels created by the white community in an effort to separate and differentiate among the various gradations of color in this growing population. The lighter-skinned octoroons sat at the top of this social scale, and "negro" or black children remained at the bottom. Although these labels were not an integral part of the vernacular of Jamaican planters and estate managers, they did appear in the slave inventories and registries from time to time; Mustiphini and Quinteroon were less common, however. When speaking of the mulatto community as a group, the white community classified everyone as mulatto. It was only when whites referred to a specific person-

TABLE 2. THE SOCIAL STRATIFICATION OF ENSLAVED CHILDREN IN JAMAICA, 1750–1834

Label	Parentage
Octoroon	Quinteroon and white parentage
Quinteroon	Mustiphini and white parentage
Mustiphini	Mustee and white parentage
Mustee	Quadroon and white parentage
Quadroon	Mulatto and white parentage
Mulatto	Negro and white parentage
Sambo	Negro and mulatto parentage
Negro	African and/or Creole 'black parentage

Sources: Madden, *Twelvemonths Residence*, 114; Phillippo, *Jamaica*, 59–60; Lewis, *Journal of a West Indian Proprietor*, 68.

in private conversation, in the slave inventories, or in Assembly matters that they used another label. Occasionally, planters and estate managers added a label to a child's name in order to differentiate him or her from the other children on the estate. It is not uncommon to see names such as Sambo John, Quadroon Sally, and Mulatto Bess among the pages of Jamaica's plantation and estate inventories during this period.

Despite the complexity of these categorizations, they overlooked the children of color who did not have a white father. Rather than create separate labels for these children, the white community occasionally classified them as *mongrels*, for instance, if a mulatto and a quadroon had a child. Some called all mulatto children mongrels, much as they labeled a dog of mixed pedigree a mongrel or a mutt. In the parish of St. David, for example, James Ouchterlong owned eleven children he classified as mongrels in the 1817 Registry of the Returns of Slaves.[42] The attachment of such a derogatory label indicates the degree to which white society devalued these children, considering them an inferior breed of slave.

Although the white community set mulatto enslaved children apart from black enslaved children, they did not completely accept these children as their own. The same was true for the enslaved population, who sometimes looked on these children with contempt. In *Marly*, a fictional account of life as a Jamaican planter written in 1828, one slave says to another, "You brown man hab no country—only de negar and de buckra hab country."[43] Some West African societies, such as the Baga of coastal Guinea, associated whiteness and albinism with evil.[44] In a society where

West Africans and their descendants were oppressed by whites, naturally those feelings only solidified in the West Indies.

Mulatto children did work in the fields, but many trained as apprentices for positions as skilled laborers, tradesmen, and domestics.[45] Once elevated to these positions, mulatto children received larger provision and clothing allowances, and some planters and estate managers reserved the most prestigious and coveted positions for their enslaved mulattos, which sparked scorn from the remaining slaves. Because enslaved domestics enjoyed a much higher status than field laborers, this resentment only intensified when slaves were expected to recognize mulatto children and adults as superior.[46] On Cornwall Estate in Westmoreland, for example, mulatto children and adults were "always honoured by their fellows with the title of Miss."[47] This worked both ways, however, as some children grew to see themselves as being a cut above the rest of the slave community.

Although their whiteness benefited and improved the health and well-being of mulatto children, Jamaican planters and estate managers also used their whiteness to measure their productivity potential. In a society that chose West Africans based on their perceived work potential and ability to withstand harsh labor and heat, whiteness became synonymous with low productivity and weakness. Planters considered mulatto children to be "weak and effeminate," quadroons "rather delicate and sickly inclined," and mustiphinis "pallid and sickly-looking."[48] Mulatto children may have been moderately valuable to the plantation economy working in the small gang as a grass picker or trash carrier, yet many planters believed that these children possessed little work potential as they grew older and joined the second and first gangs. Instead, planters and estate managers entrusted enslaved mulattos with positions that required skill and intelligence because they would be of no benefit to the plantation economy in any other capacity.

These feelings prompted some planters to manumit their enslaved mulatto children at the first available opportunity.[49] Since there were only so many domestic positions open on Jamaican estates, the enslaved mulattos who remained were sent to the fields, where they would never be seen as productive members of the labor force. In other words, planters regarded their enslaved mulattos as financial burdens, much as they had perceived enslaved children as a whole before the abolition of the slave trade. Manumitting mulatto children not only saved the planter certain expenses, such as food and clothing, but it maintained the estate's profitability by having more "able" slaves laboring in the fields. Beginning in

1774, Jamaican manumission laws stipulated that each manumitted slave must be supported by an annual annuity of five pounds colonial currency, but that meager amount did not compare to what planters spent on the general upkeep of their enslaved population.[50] Therefore, while the manumission of mulatto children seemed to be a benefit of their whiteness, it was actually an economic move on the part of the planters who adopted this practice.

Aside from believing mulattos were poor investments and unfit for field labor, some whites believed mulattos were infertile. Lady Nugent spoke for many when she declared, "Mulatto women . . . [are] constantly liable to miscarry."[51] Other whites firmly believed that mulattos could "never breed except with a separate black or white."[52] As planters increasingly relied on their enslaved children to lead them to economic stability, the breeding and work potential they expected of these children in their adulthood made them viable commodities. Combined with the belief that mulatto children were unfit for field labor, their perceived inability to produce children in their adulthood made mulatto children absolutely worthless on an estate during this later period. There was, after all, a limited need for domestic slaves. If these children could not benefit the estate as breeding wenches, then their value to the estate and the plantation economy as a whole was limited.

Although many Jamaican planters reserved the most coveted positions on their estates for their mulatto enslaved children, many of these children lived in the slave villages with the rest of the slave community. "In one family," J. B. Moreton, a Clarendon bookkeeper, wrote in 1790, "I have seen white, mestee, quadroon and mulatto children, all brothers and sisters, playing together."[53] Barry Higman has argued that mulatto children largely lived in matrifocal households with their mothers, grandmothers, and aunts, as "there was no place for slave mates in such households."[54] It is difficult to verify his claim with slave inventories and other plantation records, though some records do hint at the living arrangements of their slaves, indicating instances when "slave mates" joined a household. In 1820, for instance, Jean, a mulatto girl on Harmony Hall Estate in Vere, and her mother, Candace, moved into Adam's small thatched hut. A few years later, Candace gave birth to a "negro" girl named Kate, suggesting that Adam was the father.[55]

Contemporary observers have suggested that enslaved mulattos sought to distance themselves from the remainder of the slave community, although they lived in the slave villages. Cynric Williams, who toured Jamaica in 1823, witnessed several slave festivals where "the mulattos kept aloof, as if they disdained to mingle with the negroes." He claimed they objected to the "heathen practices of their ancestors."[56] In fact, most enslaved mulattos viewed their West African heritage as a stain on their identities as Jamaicans. By refusing to socialize with the rest of the slave community, they distanced themselves from the "negro" community, believing this brought them closer to the white community and farther away from the stereotypical "African." To borrow an image from Frantz Fanon, the mulatto community tried to "evolve" into whiteness.[57]

This evolution motivated some enslaved mulattos to follow in the footsteps of their mothers. By entering into a relationship with someone of lighter color, they too had the opportunity to improve their position on the estate. "The difference of colour . . . is a fault which no mulatto will pardon," Lewis wrote in 1817, "nor can the separation of castes in India be more rigidly observed, than that of complexional shades among the Creoles." To prove his point, Lewis gave the example of his slave Cubina. When Lewis asked him why he had not married a sambo slave named Mary Wiggins, Cubina was shocked: "Oh, massa, me black, Mary Wiggins sambo; that not allowed."[58] Although the white community created this scale of social stratification, this suggests that the slave community followed it as well. "When one of them gets a child as brown or browner than herself," Moreton wrote in 1790, "it is considered a very great blemish in her character; on the contrary, if it chances to be fairer, it is her greatest pride and glory."[59] To have a relationship with someone darker in color did not behoove a mulatto's situation at all. By entering into a relationship with someone lighter in color, however, enslaved mulattos could filter out the stain they envisioned marring their identities.

This seems to have been the case with Elizabeth Pengilly, a mulatto washerwoman attached to Thetford Plantation in the parish of St. John. Originally named Molly, Elizabeth was the daughter of a field slave named Margaretta and a white bookkeeper named William Pengilly. Pengilly left the sugar plantation sometime in 1799, the year of Molly's birth. Molly entered Thetford's small gang at age seven, two years past the normal age, but left two years later for a domestic position in the Great House. Although her mother remained in the fields, nine-year-old Molly already surpassed her in status. In 1821, by now a washerwoman on Thetford, Molly converted to Christianity and took the name Elizabeth Pengilly. While being hired out to a white man named William Thomas Fraser, Elizabeth gave birth to four quadroon children who took the name Fraser. Although William Fraser was likely the father, he terminated the contract sometime between 1827 and 1829. By 1832,

Elizabeth had given birth to two more daughters she christened as Mary and Ann Booth, quite possibly the children of Thetford's bookkeeper Edward Booth.[60]

Thetford Plantation accounts do not state whether Elizabeth Pengilly took her father's name of her own accord or at the behest of her owner. Since her father left the estate some twenty-four years earlier, it is likely that Thetford's owners did not know or care who Elizabeth's father was. They simply labeled her a mulatto and set her on the path toward domestic servitude. Perhaps Margaretta told her daughter about her father long after his dismissal from the estate, as it was Elizabeth who chose her Christian surname. What is even more interesting about Elizabeth is the personal path that she took in life. Her status as a mulatto not only made her unfit for field labor in the second gang by age nine, it also guaranteed that her future children would become Thetford domestics as well. Therefore, Margaretta's relationship with Pengilly benefited her daughter and her grandchildren. If Margaretta had taken an African or Creole "negro" slave as a partner, Elizabeth would have been categorized a "negro" and eventually would have followed her mother into the fields.

This is not to say that all mulatto children followed in their mother's footsteps. Nor is it fair to say that all mulatto children received such benefits as working in the Great House as domestics. As we have already seen, there were only so many domestic positions available on an estate. One could therefore argue that a mulatto's rise in status was made possible only by the status of their father. Since William Pengilly left Thetford Estate not long after Elizabeth's birth and was not around to ensure her removal from the children's gang for a position in the Great House, it is likely that Elizabeth's color played a greater part in her rise in status than her father's influence. As we will see, however, a father's status and influence did play a large part in their manumission. Unfortunately, Elizabeth and her children remained slaves until the abolition of slavery in 1834. That year, Elizabeth's two daughters, Ann and Mary Booth, received their freedom because they were both under the age of six.[61] Elizabeth's four children by William Fraser became apprentices alongside their mother.

Manumission, Inheritance, and Acceptance

Whereas two of Elizabeth Pengilly's children gained their freedom with the abolition of slavery in 1834, Susanna Cummings's children did not have to wait that long. A mulatto washerwoman on Worthy Park

Estate in St. John, Susanna had four quadroon children by an unknown white father. In June 1817, an unidentified party exchanged a thirteen-year-old "negro" slave named John for the manumission of Susanna's six-year-old son, Joseph. Six years later, an enslaved woman named Delia and her two children replaced Susanna and her remaining three children. It is quite possible that the father of Susanna's children arranged for their manumission. Worthy Park Estate accounts do not indicate who their benefactor was.[62]

Some fathers, especially those who were bookkeepers, could not afford to purchase slaves to exchange for their child's freedom. Although overseers averaged annual salaries of 100 to 300 pounds colonial currency, bookkeepers brought home only 30 to 80.[63] Their employers supplied them with housing and provisions, so that first year's salary usually went toward the purchase of a horse.[64] Furthermore, beginning in 1774 Jamaican law stipulated that no child could be manumitted without annual monetary support under penalty of 200 pounds colonial currency.[65] Therefore, even if a father were able to save enough money to pay the manumission fees and supply the estate with a replacement slave, he often would not have been able to provide for his child after his or her freedom.[66]

Other fathers simply chose to leave their children in a state of slavery. As was common with so many fathers of illegitimate children, many Englishmen felt it unnecessary to acknowledge their child's existence. Thistlewood fathered as many as five children during his tenure in Jamaica, but he chose to recognize only one publicly.[67] Some might give their son or daughter extra provisions or clothing when needed, but their acceptance of their children rarely went any further. Others accepted those children who were light-skinned and able to pass as white, but rejected those of a darker complexion. One such man, it was rumored, mutilated the face of his mulatto mistress in 1765 because she had a child "rather too dark."[68] Thistlewood, however, not only freed his son by Phibbah not long after his second birthday, but he provided young John with an education, a carpentry apprenticeship in his teens, and permission to join the colored militia when he became of age.[69] As the acknowledged and supported son of an Englishman, John Thistlewood's future was filled with possibility. Had he lived past the age of twenty, who knows what he would have become. However, he was the exception to the rule; most children of white men remained enslaved and ignored.

Unconcerned with public opinion or color, some fathers sought to manumit their children no matter the cost. In May 1774, John

Concannon, an overseer on Hope Estate in St. Andrew, approached one of the estate's attorneys about the manumission of his mulatto infant son, John. With an offer to supply Hope Estate with an able adult male in John's place, the attorney advised the estate's owner, the Duchess of Chandos, to accept the proposal "for Such Children are Seldom serviceable to an Estate, from the Indulgence they get when Young, besides the able Negro would be a present Advantage."[70] The duchess did not consent, and Concannon made the request again five years later, in March 1779. This time he carefully composed a letter to the duchess himself, stating briefly that he had "Reason to think the Child nearly related to me."[71] With no word from her, Concannon sent another letter, identical in tone and content, two months later. Again, the duchess sent no reply. Determined in his efforts, he sent a more forceful request in January 1780: "I will with pleasure pay whatever he may be valued at his being my son makes me impatient to have him manumised."[72] In March of that year, the duchess finally agreed to free the boy.[73] By the time of his manumission, Concannon's son was six years old.

Other fathers made similar requests, only to be denied. In April 1794, York Estate's bookkeeper John Whittaker composed a letter to the estate's attorneys requesting the freedom of his five-year-old mustee son and the mulatto son of the overseer John Waugh. Although Whittaker did not offer two slaves in exchange for the children, he argued that he wished to send his son to a school in England "for if he is kept longer in this Country, I am sorry to say, he will imbibe such bad Habits and Customs, that will be very hard to get the better of." The attorneys sent Whittaker a polite reply in August. While they empathized with his situation and that of his friend, the estate simply could not spare the two children. It was Whittaker's duty to purchase new Africans for the estate periodically, and as he had failed to do so the number of slaves had decreased in 1793. Therefore, the estate's trustees "have it not in their Power to do anything of the Kind which they are sorry for."[74]

Both Concannon's and Whittaker's experiences speak volumes of the difficulties surrounding the manumission process in Jamaica. Although some fathers owned their children and could easily grant their freedom, fathers like Concannon and Whittaker had to contact their child's owners and request permission. Sometimes this request was a mere formality. When Thistlewood contacted John and Mary Cope about the manumission of his son, John, the Copes granted his request free of charge.[75] Thistlewood's relationship with the Copes was close, however, and John Cope himself allegedly had at least one child by his slave mistress Coobah, who was the daughter of Thistlewood's mistress of thirty-three years, Phibbah.[76] More often, as we saw with Concannon's request, authorization took much longer. Although Concannon's son gained his freedom, it took six long years before the Duchess of Chandos granted that request. Perhaps she disagreed with his choice to accept his illegitimate son. As already noted, Lady Nugent often voiced her distaste for what she considered to be "licentious" relationships and noted with disgust that some were "daughters of Members of the Assembly, officers, &c. &c."[77] It is also possible that the duchess felt that Concannon should have respected his position of authority rather than enter into a relationship with one of her slaves. Unfortunately, her letter gives little insight into her reasoning.

Some children never knew how close they came to freedom. Although Whittaker received his answer in just four short months, the reply brought disappointment. Both he and Waugh never made their requests again, and their children remained slaves on York Estate. Perhaps the fathers gave up without a fight. Or they may have seen this initial request as being the only one they were obligated to make. Other fathers inquired about obtaining the freedom of their children, but were unwilling to take the necessary steps to manumit. That was certainly the case with one man who requested his mulatto daughter's freedom in 1820. That year, Hermitage Estate management conditionally granted Mr. Bonthorne's request for his daughter's freedom, provided that he supply an able field slave in her place. Although the task seemed an easy one, Bonthorne was not so inclined, and his daughter remained a slave on the St. Elizabeth estate.[78]

Men like Bonthorne and Whittaker aside, some fathers went beyond manumitting their children by arranging for inheritances of money, livestock, small pieces of property, and even slaves. As more and more fathers added codicils to their wills providing for their mulatto children, the Jamaican Assembly placed limits on the amount of property and value of the gifts that could be given. By leaving property to their children, these men announced to the world that they not only accepted their mulatto children but considered them equal to any white child. Owning property and gaining wealth raised the social status of members of the mulatto community and moved them farther away from the stigmas attached to the slave community.

Inheritance, however, complicated the boundaries between the white community and the rest of Jamaican society. According to Daniel Livesay, inheritance was "a possible time bomb that could eventually destroy white economic hegemony."[79] As a result, the Jamaican Assembly took action to keep the mulatto community firmly attached to their rung of the social ladder. In December 1761, the Assembly passed the Drummond Act, "an Act to prevent the inconveniences arising from exorbitant grants and devises to Negroes, and the issue of Negroes; and to restrain and limit such grants and devises." Effective immediately, all inheritances and monetary awards dropped from £2,000 sterling to £1,200.[80] According to Edward Long and James Phillippo Mursell, both contemporary historians of Jamaica, the law also restricted Jamaicans of color from owning sugar and coffee estates.[81] The effect of this new law went beyond restricting inheritance.[82] By limiting the amount of money and property a child inherited, the law attempted to reduce and devalue the privileges enjoyed by free blacks and free people of color, and reminded them of their inferiority to the whites of the island in the process.

The Jamaican Assembly designed the law to check the gifts that whites could bequeath to free blacks and free people of color, but the Drummond Act extended to the gifts left by nonwhites to their own children. However, individuals could petition the Assembly for immunity from the inheritance cap, and, according to Livesay, those privileges were usually granted to whites and wealthy Jamaicans of color.[83] When Samuel Strayer, a free man of color, asked the Assembly "whether the act . . . doth extend to persons of [his] description," they answered by rejecting his 1810 petition to leave a modest inheritance to his four children.[84] Focusing their attention on the inheritance potential of the colored children of the white community and wealthy Jamaicans of color, the Assembly nipped the social and economic advancement of the remaining mulatto community in the bud. By including the wills and gifts made by free people of color to their children in this law, the Assembly intended to gradually push the entire mulatto community into a lower position of limited economic standing. This allowed the Assembly and the elite to control a class of people they continually struggled to marginalize.[85] The property and money that could not be left to the children of free blacks and free people of color would be sold back to the white community at auction, further cementing the white community's position of control and superiority.

Despite the passage of the Drummond Act in 1761, some challenged the system. According to Livesay, petitions for privilege skyrocketed after the passage of the inheritance cap, and nineteen petitioners successfully lobbied the Assembly for immunity.[86] A few whites petitioned the Jamaican Assembly for exceptions, requesting that they be allowed to dispose of their estate as they saw fit. The Assembly granted John Angwin's 1787 request to leave a substantial inheritance to his four children, as long as they received an education in England and remained there for life.[87] George Bedward's request to leave his free quadroon grandson part of his estate on November 13, 1790, passed that same day.[88] Other whites chose to split their estates and property between more than one party in the same family. In 1778, the physician John Quier left six slaves to his mulatto grandsons John Quier Davis and Peter Quier Davis. To their mother, Catherine Quier, he left Shady Grove Estate, which was to be a joint possession of Catherine and another woman, named Catherine Ann Smith.[89] By granting them joint ownership of his property and slaves, Quier bypassed the Drummund Act by reducing the amount of property inherited by each mulatto listed in his will.

Others challenged the system by forcing their children and grandchildren to enter into relationships with white men or freedmen of a lighter complexion. In 1826, Frances Mackie of Westmoreland stipulated in her will that her granddaughter Ann Delap, lately manumitted, would receive an inheritance only if she became the mistress of a "creditable white person" or married "any descent person of colour."[90] Fearing that Delap would never escape the stigma of slavery if she associated with men of her color or darker, Mackie threatened Delap with poverty unless she complied with her wishes. It is unknown whether Delap followed her grandmother's wishes.

In 1813, the Jamaican Assembly repealed the Drummond Act, enabling mulattos to inherit a maximum sum of £2,000 sterling.[91] Interestingly, this was the same amount withdrawn by the Drummond Act in 1761. The repeal signified a shift in public opinion toward mulatto children. By allowing mulattos to inherit more money and more property, the Assembly enabled children of color to improve their economic standing and status in Jamaican society. Also in 1813, the Assembly passed a law allowing people of color to offer testimony in cases against members of the white community.[92] According to Livesay, the repeal of the Drummond Act resulted from effective lobbying by wealthy Jamaicans of color, who presented a stronger united front than individual petitions allowed. This strong united front looked beyond class and welcomed other members of the mulatto community to join the struggle, and the Assembly acquiesced to their petition for an appeal of the law. Livesay reports that over two thousand Jamaicans signed the petition.[93] Thus empowered, a full-fledged civil rights campaign spanned the years between 1813 and 1830, despite planter resistance and disapproval.[94] The early nineteenth century clearly witnessed a shift in opinion about the mulatto community in general, as the white community reduced the gap between whites and free people of color. At the same time, however, Jamaican law still limited the amount inherited by free people of color; whites may have lowered the glass ceiling, but they did not remove it entirely. As a result, these limitations on inheritance maintained the lower economic status of the free black and free mulatto communities and continued to keep them at bay.

Summary

Anyone possessing at least one parent of African descent suffered instant inferiority to the white community. In order to uphold that inferiority, whites living in Jamaica imposed a number of restrictions and laws that maintained distance and hegemony. Although there were laws in existence on the island that granted manumission to octoroon slaves based on their whiteness, as well as laws that allowed enslaved mulattos and freedmen to inherit property and slaves, some members of the white community refused to accept them as equals. Instead, whites in Jamaica stressed that even those "thirty generations distant from blacks blood, cannot be real whites."[95] In fact, the contemporary historian and planter Edward Long declared that "twenty or thirty generations, would hardly be sufficient to discharge the stain."[96] No matter how white a mulatto child was, that child would always be a child of color in the eyes and hearts of the white population. That "stain" so visible to the white community was enough to prohibit mulatto children from receiving the same privileges as white children well into the postemancipation period.

Although mulatto children did not receive equal privileges in their freedom, many enjoyed a higher standard of living as slaves; their whiteness enabled them to obtain better and more privileged positions on their estates and plantations, which benefited their own health and well-being as well as the health and well-being of their future children. At the same time, however, planters perceived that whiteness as a deficiency of sorts that inhibited their potential as field laborers. Therefore, although their whiteness elevated the social status of enslaved mulatto children, it devalued their worth as an economic investment as laborers and breeders. While enslaved children as a whole became important investments in the Jamaican plantation economy during this time, mulatto children remained financial burdens to the island's planters. As a result planters began to perceive enslaved mulatto children as an obstacle in their goals of economic stability and natural increase.

Thus mulatto children complicated planter ideas of slave childhood during a time when enslaved children changed from burden to investment. As planters increasingly acknowledged that enslaved children would grow up to be productive adults and lead them to economic stability and profit, most failed to recognize the enslaved children on their estates as children. Instead they perceived enslaved children only a means of protecting and securing the plantation economy. Although they were young, enslaved children were still chattel. Yet, while planters increasingly saw the mulattos on their estates as less than perfect slaves, many whites on the island began to accept them as their sons and daughters, nieces and nephews, and grandchildren, recognizing their identity as children apart from their identity as slaves. As we shall see, the introduction of Christianity to the slave villages would further influence and change the nature of slavery and childhood.

3 / "Train up a child in the way he should go": Childhood and Education in the Jamaican Slave Community

In 1798, Reverend Rees of Kingston preached a sermon on the advantages of the religious socialization of children "both to themselves and to the community." Quoting Proverbs 22:6, Rees argued that every slave owner in Jamaica should take complete responsibility in raising the enslaved children on their estates and to "train up a child in the way he should go." By learning labor skills as well as the ways of Christian morality and chastity, enslaved children could lead Jamaican planters to a future of labor security. Christian education would guarantee a docile, civilized labor force in the future. Otherwise, Reverend Rees reasoned, enslaved children would simply grow to imitate their savage parents.[1]

As we have seen, however, Jamaican planters were more concerned with the production and profit of their estates during this early period of study. "With respect to the children," Jesse Foot wrote in 1792, "as long as the mothers take care of them—they can never be in better hands." Only if the mothers died or neglected their children should the children be placed in a "publick seminary for training them in health and inclining their minds to morality and chastity." Foot said nothing about bringing Christianity to the slave community, and neither did any of his peers. For the time being, the slave community was free to raise enslaved children as they saw fit within the constraints of their situation.[2]

Past scholars have argued that the horrors of the slave trade, alienation from natal kin, and distance from those who were culturally similar destroyed African cultural traditions and beliefs, creating a new creolized slave community.[3] However, new historiographical trends are beginning to show otherwise.[4] This chapter begins by analyzing the extent to which West African cultural traditions were lost, changed, or reinvented once enslaved Africans became entrenched in a new environment. I examine the role of children as agents in the creation of the cultural landscape in Jamaican slave society before and after the abolition of the slave trade. I then explore the influence of Christianity on those cultural traditions and beliefs to see how children's roles in the slave community and the plantation complex itself changed during the nineteenth century. As we will see, while enslaved children played a minor role in the development of an African cultural identity in Jamaica, their role changed during this period of growing abolitionism as Jamaican planters welcomed Christianity into the slave villages.

Ethnic Diversity and the Jamaican Slave Community

Before the abolition of the slave trade, Jamaican enslaved children were influenced by the diverse and ever-changing language, folklore, spirituality, aesthetics, and food. Table 3 shows that slave importation trends to Jamaica fluctuated throughout the years of the slave trade.[5] Traditions from the Gold Coast and the Bight of Benin were dominant in the early seventeenth century, and in the early eighteenth century increased importations from the Bight of Biafra added their influence. According to Barry Higman, approximately 83 percent of the enslaved population in Jamaica from 1792 to 1807 came from the Bight of Biafra and Central Africa.[6] So, while new West African cultural groups were integrated into more dominant groups already entrenched on the island, other cultural groups coexisted as distinct entities alongside them. Until 1807, this constant influx of enslaved Africans created an opportunity for African cultural identities to survive, although the degree to which those traditions were maintained and reinvented is much debated today.

Archival and contemporary sources suggest that some slaves embraced their ethnic diversity. When the English abolitionist and Igbo freedman Olaudah Equiano visited Kingston in 1772, the slave community impressed him with their ability to define and maintain their national identity under slavery. "Here, each different nation of Africa meet and dance after the manner of their own country," he wrote, "[and] they still retain most of their native customs."[7] The Baptist missionary James Mursell Phillippo unwittingly confirmed the maintenance of the West African tradition of call and response when he described songs sung by enslaved women, "one alternately

TABLE 3. REGIONAL PERCENTAGES OF AFRICANS IMPORTED INTO JAMAICA, 1701–1808

Region	1701–25	1726–50	1751–75	1776–1800	1801–8
Senegambia	5.3	3.1	2.0	0.9	0.4
Sierra Leone	0.6	1.2	6.0	5.8	3.2
Windward Coast	1.0	1.0	10.9	3.1	2.4
Gold Coast	45.7	27.2	31.8	25.2	21.2
Bight of Benin	33.8	9.2	10.8	6.5	4.8
Bight of Biafra	1.6	32.3	30.0	41.3	48.8
West Central Africa	10.9	25.9	9.6	18.8	20.3
Slaves in sample	55,709	39,812	184,409	268,678	59,914

Source: Eltis, "The Volume and Structure of the Transatlantic Slave Trade," 46.

singing, while her companions repeated in chorus."[8] Other observers wrote that their slaves formed exclusive groups based on their ethnicity. Each of these groups staged dances, sang songs, wrestled, "and sometimes [played] games particular to their country."[9] The historian and planter Edward Long noted that his slaves played *warri*, a West African game of chance that taught children the fundamentals of basic mathematics.[10]

While ethnic regrouping served as a means of maintaining and reinventing the cultural traditions, beliefs, and practices of a particular ethnic group on the island, it also provided enslaved Jamaicans with a means of surviving their new life as chattel. Stephen Fuller, agent for Jamaica, wrote in 1794 that their "greatest joy is in frequent arrivals from Africa," which they saw as a means of connecting with those of a similar ethnic background.[11] As we have already seen, some Africans coped with their life as slaves by forming new kinship groups. "They will instantly make acquaintances," the Jamaican planter William Beckford wrote in 1788, "or form connections with those who have been before purchased from their own country."[12] By forming kin-like affiliations with other slaves of the same ethnic group who shared similar beliefs and practices, enslaved Africans found a way of maintaining or reinventing their national identity in a new environment so far away from home. According to Douglas B. Chambers, a new national identity formed where slaves who were collectively called *eboe* or *coromontee* created a new culture out of collective memories of their West African Igbo or Akan culture.[13]

As West Africans struggled to maintain their national identity under slavery, a multiplicity of cultural traditions, practices, and beliefs from these diverse ethnic groups imported into the island gradually combined to form what many planters and estate managers recognized as an "African" culture. Because planters and estate managers were more concerned with the work potential of their slaves rather than their personal lives, the slave community had some control over the degree to which they practiced their traditions and beliefs, giving them the power to negotiate their own cultural identity and educate their children in the way that they saw fit.

African Cultural Identity

Defining the place of children in this complex cultural landscape is difficult. We do not know how a multiethnic background shaped the self-perception of these children, or if it did at all. Some children identified with their parents' shipmates as family or kin; others became part of an adopted family or kinship group. Some parents encouraged their mulatto children to reject their West African heritage in an attempt to assimilate themselves into English society; others simply raised their children in the manner in which they themselves were raised, as eboe and coromontee, African, colored, or Creole.

The existing sources do indicate that some parents tried to maintain specific West African cultural traditions and practices, beginning with choosing their children's names, which carried spiritual significance. Archival sources indicate that enslaved children in Jamaica occasionally received West African day names, as was customary in Akan, Ga, and Ewe cultures, where children were named after the day of their birth.[14] According to Jamaican folklore, certain names carried more weight than others: Wednesday-born children named Quaco and Cuba were perceived as lucky, whereas Friday-born children named Cuffee and Phibbah were unlucky. Superstition followed Monday-born children, as it was commonly believed that events taking place on Mondays followed one through the remainder of the week.[15] In a comparison between Akan and Jamaican names in Table 4, changes in spelling suggest the bookkeeper recording the names in the inventories spelled them phonetically. Names like Friday and Tuesday as well as January and December also make appearances in the slave inventories, albeit in limited numbers. Although we cannot be sure that these names were given by the child's parents, their occasional appearance suggests the day name tradition was being reinvented by the slave community.

TABLE 4. AKAN DAY NAMES IN JAMAICA

Day	Akan Male Name	Jamaican Male Name	Akan Female Name	Jamaican Female Name
Sunday	Kwasi, Kwashi	Quashie	Kwasheba, Akosua	Quasheba
Monday	Kojo, Cudjoe	Cudjoe	Juba, Adua	Juba
Tuesday	Kwamina, Kwabena	Cubbenah	Beneba, Abena	Benebah
Wednesday	Kwaku, Kwaco	Quaco	Kuba, Akua	Cuba
Thursday	Yao, Kwao	Quao	Aba, Yaa	Abba
Friday	Kofi, Cuffee	Cuffee	Afua, Fiba	Phibba
Saturday	Kwame, Kwamin	Quamin	Mimba, Amba, Ama	Mimba

Sources: Gardner, *A History of Jamaica*, 183; Warner-Lewis, "The Character of African-Jamaican Culture," 90.

Equiano remembered that children in his village of Isseke, located in present-day Nigeria, were often named "from some event, some circumstance, or fancied foreboding, at the time of their birth."[16] That tradition possibly endured in Jamaica as well, as plantation and estate inventories list children with names like Hardtimes, Badhead, Smallhope, and Littleworth.[17] Again, we do not know whether these children received their names from their parents or from the estate managers and bookkeepers; we do know that some enslaved Jamaicans did have the power to name their own children and others did not. Names like these may indicate that parents were using traditional naming practices, or they may illustrate how planters as well as slaves felt about children in the slave community.

In January 1824, a Radnor Estate bookkeeper noted in the estate's inventories that George and Grace's young daughter Moriah died of worms; the following year, a slave woman named Elfrida gave birth to a daughter whom she named Moriah. Interestingly, just two years earlier in 1823, Elfrida's daughter Grace had died of yaws. We do not know whether the parents were naming their children in honor of another slave or if the Radnor Estate managers or owners had a decided interest in the names Grace and Moriah. In other parts of the Americas, for example, when a slave died, the owner simply gave the next newborn the dead person's name. This helped planters and estate managers remember the names of their slaves and avoid the duplication of names. In Jamaica, however, planters occasionally duplicated the names of their slaves on their estates. In the Registry of the Returns of Slaves, for example, it was not uncommon for bookkeepers to list two or three slaves named Bess or Sam.[18] Radnor Estate inventories do not duplicate the names of slaves, nor do they state whether Grace and Elfrida were related, yet the names propose the real possibility of some sort of bond existing between the two enslaved women.[19]

In contrast, some slaves avoided certain ancestral names for fear of harming their child. On Cornwall Estate in Westmoreland, for example, a Creole man named Neptune requested that his son's name be changed from Oscar to Julius. "The child, he said, had always been weakly," Lewis, owner of the estate, wrote in 1817, "and he was persuaded that its ill health proceeded from his deceased grandfather's being displeased because it had been called after him." Another woman on Cornwall Estate approached Lewis with a similar request. Her daughter Lucia lay sick in the estate hothouse, and she "begged me to change its name for any other which might please me best." If the child continued to be named Lucia, the child's mother believed, she would surely die. Unfortunately, Lucia's mother does not explain why her daughter's name carried so much significance, nor do we know whether Lewis granted her request. Perhaps it was the name of an angry ancestor, as was the case with Neptune. Whatever the reason, it seems that enslaved Creoles continued to believe that children's names carried spiritual significance long after the abolition of the slave trade.[20]

Not every parent had the power to name their children themselves. Some planters named enslaved children after famous persons in English history or literature, such as Oliver Cromwell and Shakespeare, or after English cities like Bristol, Oxford, and Cambridge. On Thetford Estate in the parish of St. John, like many others on the island, bookkeepers listed the names of the estate's enslaved children with their mother's names attached, such as Eve's Diligence, Amelia's Cassandra, and Pomelia's Cuffee.[21] Other planters attached degrees of whiteness to their enslaved children's names, such as Mulatto Bess and Quadroon Sam, as a means of separating these children from the rest of enslaved population. Trevor Burnard argues that such slave names are more a window into how planters perceived their slaves than "an entrée into slave consciousness."[22] While some names assisted children in developing an identity apart from their English owners or fellow slaves, other names served as constant reminders that they were slaves first and children second.

Despite English influence and planter control, there is a significant presence of African day names surviving into the nineteenth century. Even in 1817 the Registry of the Returns of Slaves lists Creole enslaved children, often of Creole parentage, with names such as Cuba, Cudjoe, Quaw, and Beneba. Two Creole women of African parentage on two different estates in the parish of Westmoreland named their children Eboe and Fantee. In the parish of St. George, the returns listed a twenty-eight-year-old Creole woman named Banda.[23] This suggests that these mothers wanted their children to understand who they were, as well as where their ancestors came from. Names like these gave children an identity outside of their identity as slaves and educated them about their past, ensuring that their national identity was protected from the destructive process of slavery.

From the time enslaved children received their names, they absorbed certain traditions, beliefs, and practices from a variety of outlets, of which folklore was the most pervasive. As in many West African societies, folklore was and still is a tool used in daily life to teach children respect, caution, bravery, courage, perseverance, and morality.[24] As these traditions crossed the Atlantic, however, enslaved Jamaicans modified them to fit their new surroundings and experiences. More important, these reinvented folklore traditions educated a new generation of children, a generation that was born into slavery. Jamaican riddles, for example, occasionally included images of the slave trade. One riddle asked children to guess what resembled a "guinea ship full of people who came out with red coats & black heads."[25] The answer was *ackee*, derived from the Twi word *ankye*, a black-seeded fruit inside a large red pod that was brought to the island by a West African slave ship in 1788.[26] Riddles such as these enhanced memory skills and also taught the children about their heritage. Sayings from the period, such as "Every John Crow think him pickney white," touch on the elevated status of mulatto children in Jamaican slave society. A few West African sayings and proverbs managed to survive the slave experience. When Jamaicans today say "Bad family betta dan empty pigsty," they echo a sentiment expressed in Ghana: "A bad person is better than an empty house."[27] The survival of sayings like these is evidence that certain West African educational traditions did not disappear during the slave era.

Enslaved Jamaicans likely taught their children moral lessons through stories and fables as well. Largely featuring animals such as spiders, crabs, monkeys, and snakes, West African stories and fables traveled across the Atlantic in various forms, but all stressed certain moral messages and explanations. Thomas Thistlewood related one tale told to him in 1751 by a Coromontee slave woman about a monster called Cokroyamkou who waited in the shadows to eat children after they fell asleep.[28] Cokroyamkou's presence in Jamaica illustrates the slave community's need to explain the infant and child mortality plaguing the slave villages and also shows the tenacity of such legends and stories. Although no other contemporary source mentions the monster in relation to infant and child death, no other contemporary figure apart from Thistlewood took the time to discuss such issues with their slaves or preserve their existence in their diaries.

After enlightening Thistlewood with the legend of Cokroyamkou, that same Coromontee slave woman told him the story of an old woman who refused to give her grandchild meat unless he could say her name. The child did not know his grandmother's name, and he nearly starved to death. One day he met a crab who told him to say "Osissi, O Ninni O Barrebanshante Jamande" to his grandmother at their next meeting. That evening, as she tormented him about the meat, the boy spoke the magic words and received his portion. Thanks to the crab, his life was saved.[29]

A similar story appears in Ga folklore. In this story, a hippo regularly invited friends to feast at his home but refused to share his food unless they guessed his name. A tortoise, determined to share in the feast, followed the hippo one day and overheard his wife speak his name. At the next feast, the tortoise revealed the hippo's secret and each guest took part in the feast. This story may have been the basis for the one Thistlewood's slave related to him. The moral of the story remained the same, though the characters changed to reflect the new environment. Stories like these taught children and adults alike self-sufficiency in case they found themselves orphaned, without their kinship group, or sold to another estate.[30]

Such stories, otherwise known as Anansi, Anancy, or Nancy stories, fill Jamaican folklore and are still told to children today. Named after the infamous spider trickster Anansi who wreaked havoc along the Gold Coast of West Africa, the stories made their way across the Atlantic to entertain and educate Jamaican enslaved children before they went off to bed. In 1817, Lewis recorded in his journal, "The Negroes are very fond of what they call Nancy stories, part of which is related and part sung." Lewis described two stories that did not contain Anansi as the main character but noted that his slaves considered them Nancy stories nonetheless.[31] It is quite possible that enslaved Jamaicans eventually called all of their folktales Nancy stories, whether the stories were of Igbo, Akan, or Mandingo origin.

According to Emily Zobel Marshall, Anansi stories played a multifunctional role, instilling a sense of continuity with the cultural traditions left behind while offering enslaved Africans and their children the means to assert and negotiate their identity in Jamaica.[32] While all of these stories contain a moral message, the background and characters changed to reflect new social issues and problems, revealing a need to survive and endure in an oppressive and dangerous environment by keeping connections to Africa as alive as possible. The style of the stories changed as well, incorporating narrative as well as song.[33] With each generation, these stories became less African and more Jamaican. Although we have a general idea of how Jamaican enslaved children related to the folklore traditions of their past, our knowledge of their cultural development outside of that is rather limited. Aside from folklore, the relationship of other cultural traditions, beliefs, and practices to Jamaican enslaved children are even more difficult to pinpoint. While planters and estate managers detail other cultural survivals and reinventions in the areas of food, music, funeral practices, and spiritual beliefs, they fail to discuss how children related to these traditions.[34] So, we do not know the degree to which they retained these beliefs and passed them down to their own children, nor do we know how they participated in these aspects of African-Jamaican culture. Despite these limitations, we do have an idea how children related to the ethnic diversity of the slave community in terms of language. Despite the fact that planters expected their slaves to learn English, archival sources indicate that some enslaved children held on to African languages. In his research on the slave trade to Jamaica, Douglas B. Chambers describes the case of a boy named Brutus who fled his plantation in Black River, St. Elizabeth in 1791 for parts unknown. In the advertisement that appeared in the *Royal Gazette* after Brutus's escape, his owner stated that he "calls himself a Creole, but is supposed to be from Africa, as he talks both the Eboe and Coromantee languages very fluently." In his analysis of the runaway, Chambers posited that perhaps Brutus was born in Africa and learned another West African language in Jamaica while retaining his own. Or maybe Brutus was a Creole and had parents from both the Bight of Biafra and the Gold Coast who passed their languages down to him. Since these two languages were in everyday use alongside English in late eighteenth-century Jamaica, Brutus's case exemplifies the complex cultural environment in which enslaved children lived during this period.[35]

The complexities of Brutus's situation allude to the development of multilingualism among Jamaican enslaved children. As a multiplicity of West Africans poured into Jamaican ports before the abolition of the slave trade, enslaved children had access to a wide variety of languages. Some, like Brutus, became bilingual and even multilingual. Others grew up speaking English and nothing more. After the abolition of the slave trade, however, the nature of language in Jamaica changed. As the Creole population grew to outnumber the African population on the island, Jamaican patois became the lingua franca of the enslaved population.[36] As we have already seen, ethnic diversity developed in the Jamaican slave villages as the slave trade shifted importation trends. Since the slave community lacked a common language, the various West African languages spoken in the slave villages combined with the English of their owners and estate managers to create Jamaican patois.

According to the linguists Frederick Cassidy and Robert Le Page, despite increased imports of slaves from West Central Africa during the last years of the trade, the Akan- and Ewe-speaking peoples imported into the island before 1800 firmly established their dialects in this new language. Although these dialects provided a platform for the development of Jamaican patois, Cassidy and Le Page also note that patois itself had its own dialectical variations dependent on the ethnic dispersal of slaves to Jamaica's estates.[37] For example, while all enslaved Jamaicans used the Igbo word *buckra* to describe the white men on their estates, other words became more parish-specific or had different meanings in different parishes.[38] Slaves in Kingston and St. Andrew used the Ewe word *talawah* for "strength," whereas it came to mean "stubbornness" in St. Mary.[39] English words became part of Jamaican patois as well. *Pickaninny*, used by planters and estate managers to describe enslaved children, evolved into *pickney*. Even today, one occasionally hears the word in Jamaican conversation. Just as ethnic diversity influenced the development of Jamaican patois in the slave community, the demographic composition of the island played a part as well. Mulatto and urban enslaved children learned a dialect with more English intonations, syntax, and vocabulary because of their close contact with the white community, and rural enslaved children living on estates with one or two white men learned a patois that was less influenced by English and more an amalgam of African sounds and words.

Whereas Jamaican enslaved children heard and often spoke a variety of languages in the slave villages, planters and estate managers believed that children began "adopting the African words [more] for ease of communication."[40] What most likely occurred, however, is that enslaved children began to use the language that was more functional for them.

Like Brutus, many children understood the languages their parents spoke and even spoke those languages at home to their parents and kin. Daily life on the estates, however, required a greater usage of English and patois; therefore, these two languages took precedence on Jamaican plantations. As Jamaican patois became more prevalent in the slave community after the abolition of the slave trade, however, children like Brutus likely became more exceptional than ordinary.

Contemporary sources suggest that, whether speaking three languages or only one, many Creole and African children addressed their parents much in the same way as they did on the other side of the Atlantic. W. J. Gardner and Robert Renny, both residents and historians of Jamaica during this period, noted that many enslaved children used the words *ta* and *ma* to address their parents and elders.[41] According to Maureen Warner-Lewis, the practice of using *ta* and *ma* is still considered a necessary aspect of social etiquette in many West African societies.[42] The continuation of such expressions in Jamaican slave society suggests that the value of respect for elders continued under slavery. Teaching their children to call their elders *ta* and *ma* was simply a part of their upbringing, much like the usage of *sir* and *ma'am* in the U.S. South today.

Other cultural practices specifically relating to children did not survive in Jamaica. On June 19, 1765, Thistlewood purchased ten Africans while serving as overseer of Egypt Estate in Westmoreland. Four of those slaves were children under fifteen. Chub, a boy about thirteen, had "3 perpindicular scars down each Cheek," and Damsel was a "Chambry Woman Girl" about the same age who had "on her face 3 long strokes down each Cheek . . . her belly full of Country Marks, & an Arch between her Breasts."[43] Marks such as these fascinated Jamaican planters, who understood that besides being "highly ornamental . . . they are said to indicate free birth and honourable parentage."[44] In Igbo culture, for example, these marks were given only to relatives and descendants of the elders and leaders of the community.[45] One of Thistlewood's favorite slave paramours, Nago Jenny, told him in 1752 that before she was kidnapped as a child from her parents' home, she received similar marks because "she was a grande Man's Pickinniny."[46]

Like Nago Jenny, the African children who arrived in Jamaica received these marks to signify their status in their kinship groups and communities. Rituals such as these failed to survive the slave experience. Perhaps elders in the slave community found it impossible to perform such social rituals in an environment that negated the development of family hierarchies. Furthermore, these "country marks" often coincided with certain tasks and rites performed by the child in an initiation into adulthood that occurred shortly after puberty. Aside from a lack of free time to perform these rituals, the responsibilities and rights that were commonplace in West Africa could not be perpetuated once West Africans were taken outside of their societies and enslaved.

Social Control and Child Socialization

So far I have focused mainly on the ethnic diversity of the slave community and the transference of their cultural practices, traditions, and beliefs to children. While we have seen how children related to the development of a cultural landscape in Jamaica, great difficulty lies in discovering what these children retained and passed along to their own children. Certain beliefs and traditions were transferred to children, but the amount of what was transferred changed over time, and it is likely that children played a very small role in that process, especially after the abolition of the slave trade. As abolitionist sentiment increased, enslaved children became important to the plantation complex as an investment. Once English abolitionists succeeded in ending the English trade, they focused their attention on the institution of slavery itself. Consequently Jamaica planned for a future without slaves. Terrified to live on an island populated with "ignorant savages" who failed to understand their subordinate place in society, planters envisioned children as their salvation, and the nature of childhood in Jamaica changed yet again. Before the abolition of the slave trade, Jamaican planters opposed any formal instruction for slaves, children included. Suspicious of outside influence from missionaries, the planter elite saw religious education as a subversive force rather than a controlling one. When they converted to Christianity, the enslaved population received a new view of the world, in which ideas of equality and hope challenged their present situation. Black missionaries like George Leile, a freedman from Savannah who migrated to Jamaica in the 1780s, were proof that freedom was a possibility if one accepted God. Comprising only 10 percent of the total population, Jamaican planters saw little hope for safety from a religiously charged enslaved population that had a history of violent revolt.[47] For that reason, the Jamaican Assembly passed a law in 1802 restricting missionaries not "duly qualified by law."[48] Five years later, the Assembly amended the Consolidated Slave Law by outlawing all non-Anglican missionaries from the island, knowing full well that there were very few Anglican missionaries in Jamaica.[49] Therefore, with little influence from planters, enslaved Jamaicans had the power to raise their children as they saw fit.

By 1815, however, Jamaican planters had changed their tune. Nearly a decade after the abolition of the Atlantic slave trade, the enslaved population still failed to reproduce naturally at a rate planters and estate managers needed. Furthermore, cheaper alternative sugar supplies from India in the form of beet sugar began to challenge the island's position as England's most important colony. As English abolitionists increasingly directed their energy toward the institution of slavery, Jamaican planters reevaluated their stance on the religious instruction of the enslaved population. They still mistrusted missionaries and their influence, but some felt that religious instruction of the enslaved children on their estates would rescue their own faltering position.

Although Jamaican planters felt uneasy about how religious instruction could influence their slaves' psyches, some hoped that they could use missionaries to control and manipulate their slaves. Richard Barrett, a prominent slave owner and speaker of the Jamaican Assembly, spoke for many when he told one missionary, "I have a bad set of people: they steal enormously, run away, get drunk, [and] fight." More important, their savagery threatened the very livelihood of the estate, as "the women take no care of their children and there is no increase on the property." Without the proper guidance, enslaved children would only grow to emulate their parents. Open to anything, Barrett gave the missionary ministering privileges on his estate. "If you can bring them under fear of God," Barrett told him, "you may be doing both them and me a service."[50]

Planters weren't the only ones to feel this way. Phillippo, the Baptist missionary and eight-year resident of Jamaica, lamented, "Every negro hut was a common brothel: every woman a prostitute, and every man a libertine." Polygamy ran rampant, and enslaved men controlled harems of enslaved women and girls. When he published his history seventeen years after leaving the island, he reflected on what he perceived as a state of society dripping with licentiousness. Phillippo also remembered a hyperbolic history of fourteen-year-old girls who had "sacrificed all pretentions of virtue . . . whilst hundreds were known to have become mothers before they had even entered upon their teens." Rum was given to infants as soon as they were born. The Jamaican slave community was filled with degenerates desperately in need of his guiding hand.[51]

Although most planters would agree that their slaves lived immorally, they would disagree with Phillippo's exaggerated characterization of enslaved girls' fertility. In fact, in their opinion, it was their slaves' immorality and licentiousness that prevented natural increase. Most planters would likely side with Barrett rather than Phillippo, hoping that religious education could strengthen social control, encourage productivity, and boost natural increase on their estates. Although many assemblymen and planters continued to mistrust Jamaican missionaries, the Assembly lifted the ban on non-Anglican missionaries in 1816, so long as no religious instruction or meetings took place after sundown.[52] Consequently Jamaican planters and missionaries reached an uneasy alliance; during planting and harvest, the planters allowed missionaries on their estates only if they used the scriptures to stress a Protestant work ethic and manipulate the slaves to work harder in the fields and boiling houses. The Assembly also allowed missionaries to travel the countryside, but only if they preached sermons on loyalty and subservience and taught the enslaved population that theft, unruly behavior, alcohol consumption, and promiscuity were mortal sins.

Planters, therefore, carefully used religious instruction to enhance their social control; they hoped that it would lead to improvements in low birth rates as well. Long convinced that their slaves lived in a constant state of licentiousness and promiscuity, some felt that such immorality affected their ability to reproduce. This was not a new revelation on the island, as petitions appeared before the Jamaican Assembly as early as 1799 pushing for slave marriage and baptism laws. "To multiply the human species," one petition stated in 1799, "there must be a marriage or something to that effect; a contract of this kind is actually necessary."[53] The Assembly agreed that marriage brought longevity to a couple, which made them healthier and more fertile.[54] Those slaves who did not accept Christian marriage would die young and childless.

Despite these beliefs, very few slave owners encouraged their slaves to participate in such a ceremony. For example, the first Christian slave marriage did not take place in Kingston until April 30, 1803, when Henry Brailsford and Amelia Young, both slaves in the parish, were married. Another Christian slave marriage would not take place for four years in Kingston.[55] By the 1820s, however, Christian marriage became more commonplace in the slave community as owners and missionaries increasingly urged Jamaica's slaves to enter into Christian marriages. Of the 330,000 slaves living on the island in 1825, Methodist missionaries reported to the House of Commons that a total of 2,493 marriages took place between 1821 and 1825; at Carmel and Fairfield estates Moravian missionaries performed 189 marriages between 1827 and 1834.[56] In 1840 Phillippo contended, "The ceremony has become so common as to be an almost daily occurance."[57] Some slaves married at the urging of their owners; others chose to accept the Christian ritual on their own volition. Mary Turner posits that more slaves entered into Christian marriages because it forced Jamaican planters to acknowledge and respect their family units and obligations.[58] More recent research by Nicolas M. Beasley suggests a similar motivation, proposing that Christian marriage offered slaves legitimacy and autonomy where sexuality and reproduction were concerned.[59] Whatever the motivation, missionaries believed that their influence was taking hold: "The consequent happy effects on Negro families . . . are in great part the direct effects of Missionary exertions."[60]

In order to curtail the bad influence enslaved parents had on their children, beginning in the 1810s more and more enslaved children born on the island were baptized soon after birth. Missionaries believed that baptism saved children's souls before they were marred too badly by the "savagery" of the slave villages; even greater success was achieved when they began to baptize slaves en masse by 1815.[61] In fact, as D. A. Dunkley has shown, mass baptism was a veritable business by this time.[62] On their appointed date and time, entire estate populations gathered together either at the parish or estate church. The slaves were asked their names and then quickly baptized, and the rector received a half crown colonial currency for each baptism.[63] From 1818 to 1821, for example, missionaries and parish rectors in the parish of St. Thomas in the East baptized a total of 7,470 slaves.[64] With so many baptisms taking place in the parishes St. Catherine, Hanover, and St. Dorothy between 1817 and 1825, rectors saved time by registering the names of the estates instead.[65]

In 1825, Reverend Richard Bickell boasted that he had baptized nearly one thousand slaves in the space of six months in Kingston, "with little or no examination," concerning himself more with payment than with saving souls.[66] "'It was like driving cattle to a pond,'" the missionary Hope Masterson Waddell wrote, quoting a convert. "'I heard something about God,' said another, 'but thought the parson in the long gown was he.'"[67] Waddell's complaints about the insincerities of mass baptism suggest that the process was not as consensual as missionaries thought, possibly leaving room for the continued practice of West African religious beliefs. Alleging that slaves came forward for baptism largely at their owners' urging, Waddell's criticism adds insight into these mass baptisms. While some missionaries saw their work as bringing salvation to the Godless, others saw it as a means of increasing revenue for the parish, the rectory, and themselves. From the planters' point of view, this brought them one step closer to a more prolific and fertile enslaved population. Although Jamaican planters continued to keep a watchful eye on the missionaries ministering to their slaves, many in the white community believed that it was a beneficial situation for all parties involved.

Christian marriage and mass baptism did not erase the traditions and beliefs passed down to enslaved children, however, and contemporary sources indicate that some in the slave community merely modified their practices to make room for the changes that were taking place. On Cornwall Estate in Westmoreland, for example, the slave community produced "Eboe drums" for each child's baptism and continued to educate their children as they had before by teaching them Nancy stories, proverbs, and riddles.[68] Despite the complete replacement of African day names with proper English names like Elizabeth Warren and John Wilson in estate inventories and the Registry of the Returns of Slaves by 1826, slaves continued to place spiritual significance on their children's names.[69] Lewis deferred to his slaves' wishes in what he considered to be special circumstances. One slave came to him before his son's baptism with "his heart set on calling the boy John Lewis, after his friend and myself; so John Lewis he was."[70] Being baptized and attending Sunday worship services did not mean that enslaved Jamaicans abandoned their own traditions and beliefs; it is likely that many parents continued to raise their children as they had in the past.

In the 1820s, enslaved Jamaicans witnessed a change in planter opinion toward their children. Although planters conditionally allowed missionaries to impress ideas of morality and virtue on the slave community, they took a more direct approach toward the education of enslaved children. Feeling pressure from English abolitionists bent on bringing an end to the institution of slavery, planters tried to envision a future when the laborers on their estates were free. Fearing a situation that mirrored the economic devastation that accompanied the newly independent Haiti, Jamaica planned to take preventative action by educating the island's enslaved children into a more manageable class of people in their adulthood. John Ashton Yates, a West Indian planter, wrote of enslaved children in 1824, "As long as they are merely controlled by a strict system of severity, they continue stupid and troublesome."[71] Worse yet, declared George Wilson Bridges, "children, from the most tender age, are permitted to indulge the basest instincts of their nature; their mind . . . is a waste."[72] By removing enslaved children from their parents' influence, teaching them English morals and values and to properly speak the English language, "to obey their master, and to be content in the situation in which Providence has placed them," planters hoped to avoid a disastrous transition to freedom.[73] With abolition looming on the horizon, this new generation of enslaved children grew into adulthood with a prospect of freedom unknown to previous generations in Jamaica. As the nature of slavery in Jamaica began to change yet again, new ideas of freedom began to influence planters' definitions of childhood.

A few of the more hesitant planters debated whether it was prudent to educate the children on their estates. The issue was not that enslaved children could not be educated; in fact, many claimed that the children of African descent educated alongside white children in England actually learned faster than their white classmates. Skeptics argued that education and slavery could not coexist because education was wasted on slaves; it went beyond their purpose and need, and it allowed missionaries to inject ideas of rebellion and defiance into the slave community. Devil's advocates argued, however, that education was the only way to work against the abolitionist cause. Education beat abolitionists at their own game. By teaching enslaved children to become good workers, these new and improved slaves would gradually replace the old. If abolition did come, the newly freed population would know their place and remain loyal.[74]

Although they remained apprehensive, many planters gradually took their enslaved children out of the plantation nurseries and placed them in schools, either in the towns or on the estates, where they were taught the queen's English and proper etiquette alongside free black children and free children of color. [75] Planters allowed missionaries and parish rectors to visit their estates weekly to provide enslaved children with religious instruction and services apart from the adults. As part of the curriculum in many schools, the children performed light duties around the estate from time to time. "To prevent the idea that freedom implied idleness, we established a working lesson in our school, and for an hour daily they had all to labour out of doors," Reverend Waddell. "So many little hands could do a great deal of work, of which we had at that time plenty to engage them."[76] These schools taught children how to be better, more obedient laborers before their entrance into the children's gangs, so they would be better, more productive freedmen in their adulthood. Despite increased abolitionist sentiment in England, planters began to envision a free Jamaica that was not unlike the island under slavery.

To help ensure that their plan was a success, a few schools recruited teachers from within the slave community. In 1828, for example, the St. Catherine Vestry established a school in Spanish Town specifically for this purpose.[77] Of the sixty-five children in the school that year, seven graduated as teachers and left for Ellis' Caymanas, Ellis' Crawle, Twickenham Park, Cross Pen, Worthy Park, Spring Vale, Woodlands, and Rose Hill estates.[78] There they began schools of their own under the supervision of an appointed clergyman. On rural estates, some bookkeepers instructed one or two of the most promising children so that they "might afterwards devote some of their spare hours in the evening, to teaching the young negroes."[79] By using educated children as examples, planters hoped to draw more enslaved children into the estate and parish schools. Furthermore, these educated and "assimilated" children would provide uneducated enslaved children with a role model of sorts. Education not only improved their status as slaves, but it also promised certain freedoms denied those children who remained unschooled.

Although missionaries continued to complain that planters refused to allow the religious education of the children on their estates, estate schools increased in number until the end of slavery in 1834.[80] We do not have an estimate of the number of schools or the number of enslaved children educated on the island in 1834, but George Baille, a Jamaican planter, told the House of Lords in 1832 that there was hardly a town in Jamaica that did not have a school.[81] On the eve of abolition, Jamaican planters convinced themselves that the enslaved children on their estates benefited from their religious education, despite the increased rebelliousness of the enslaved population on the island, and Jamaican missionaries concurred. When Reverend John Jenkins, a Wesleyan missionary, arrived in Jamaica in 1830, he "expected to find . . . an ignorant, depressed, and miserable set of people, whose knowledge was as little as their condition was destitute." Sent to judge the success of the Wesleyan mission in Jamaica at converting the enslaved population, Jenkins took his assignment seriously. After a thorough inspection of slaves on a few estates ministered by his peers, he was surprised to find a congregation filled with children that met the standards set by the Wesleyan mission as well as his own.[82] Not only did they sing hymns and quote scripture, but they also attended plantation schools and were baptized in the Christian faith. Whether they did this of their own free will or at the urging of their owners, it was enough to convince Jenkins that the savages he had only heard about were now a civilized group of laborers.

Summary

As the abolitionist movement changed the nature of Jamaican slavery, planters' ideas of childhood shifted yet again. While planters congratulated themselves on their success in socially conditioning their enslaved children into more profitable investments, children's roles in the plantation complex evolved with this new generation of slaves. The planters who once concerned themselves only with production and profit now became obsessed with the moral upbringing of the children on their estates. Enslaved children had become viable economic investments to the plantation economy; now planters began to attach a social value to them as well. Their evolution into "civilized" and moral commodities still attached enslaved children to the economic viability of the plantation economy, but their roles on the island shifted their identity from slave to future freedman as Jamaican planters accepted the inevitability of abolition. Consequently, education began to define freedom for the slave community, at least as much as their owners would allow.

As planters tried to erase the cultural traditions, beliefs, and practices enslaved children retained from their parents and kinship groups, the slave community witnessed a transformation in the education of their children. Despite such interference, enslaved Jamaicans struggled to raise their children as they saw fit. Although archival sources do not indicate the extent to which the children transferred what they learned to the rest of the slave community, their Christian education certainly challenged the traditions and beliefs practiced by their parents and kinship groups. As we will see, the apprenticeship period only intensified the educational conditioning of the newly freed enslaved population. Although Reverend John Barry testified before the House of Commons in 1832, "Negro children are the most dutiful and obedient children, generally speaking, that I have ever known," Sir Michael Clare, a physician practicing in Jamaica since 1802, testified that while the moral licentiousness of the enslaved population appeared to be improved, it was not.[83] Furthermore, apprenticeship intensified the ideas of freedom already formulating in the slave community. At the same time, however, one final change occurred in planter opinion toward enslaved children as the abolition of slavery in the British colonies brought the changing nature of childhood in Jamaica full circle.

4 / "That iniquitous law": The Apprenticeship and Emancipation of Jamaica's Enslaved Children

In November 1836, Stephen Hannaford, owner of several properties in the parish of St. Dorothy, petitioned the Jamaican Assembly for economic support for an orphaned infant on Top Hill Estate. For months Hannaford had supported the infant after the child's mother, an apprentice named Dolly, died. While procuring a wet nurse for the infant, he repeatedly asked the child's reputed father, the head cattleman on Hannaford's Kelly Estate, to take the baby. The father refused, so Hannaford approached Dolly's remaining family living on both estates. They too refused, and Hannaford turned to the St. Dorothy Special Magistrate for permission to take the child to a caretaker. That request denied, he appealed to the Assembly to enact a law "which would compel a father to support his reputed children." The Assembly refused, knowing such a law would set a devastating precedent in motion that would require all fathers to support their illegitimate children, no matter their color. Archival sources do not indicate what ultimately became of Dolly's infant.[1]

Although Hannaford's case was a rare one, it adds insight to the changing nature of childhood under apprenticeship. While the law stipulated that Hannaford could indenture Dolly's infant until his or her twenty-first year, he did not. To do so would mean that he still had to support an infant who would not be of working age until 1842. Hannaford needed laborers, not investments, and Dolly's orphan was a risky investment at that, since the infant's father and family refused to offer their support. As Hannaford pleaded for governmental aid to ease the financial burden this infant presented, he sought to stop this from happening to others in his position in the future. Yet, while Hannaford desperately tried to remove the child from his care, he did not just stand aside and let the child die, even though there would have been no legal penalty. Hannaford was trying to do the right thing. His frustration over the burden this infant brought to his estate's economic standing during apprenticeship is representative of how other planters felt about the changes taking place on the island and in the British Caribbean as a whole.

Although Hannaford's perception of Dolly's infant as a burden is to be expected, the reaction that came from the child's kin shows a change in the value of children in the apprentice community as well. According to apprenticeship laws, free children were the responsibility of their parents, yet, the reputed father was not willing to add another mouth to feed. His refusal shows that he too felt Dolly's infant would be a burden. Although Dolly may have worked hard to provide for her child, her family did not feel any responsibility toward the infant at all. As we will see, however, not every apprentice's family felt the same way.

With the passage of apprenticeship, planters and their apprenticed adult laborers negotiated the contours of the emerging postemancipation civil and political economy between 1833 and 1840. The most important site of these negotiations was the family, specifically the children who suddenly enjoyed full freedom. While these negotiations took place throughout the British Caribbean, Jamaica's experiences during this process serve as an excellent case study. Despite intense pressure from planters, most African-Jamaican mothers insisted on making their own fertility choices, deciding their children's fate, and bearing the costs of their children's care. With apprenticeship, planters struggled to coexist with a system that threatened economic ruin as their apprentices realized their ability to negotiate the freedom of their children. The transition to freedom not only changed the nature of African-Jamaican family life and childhood, but it redefined the relationship between black women, their employers, and the Jamaican state.

The Problem

As we have already seen, Jamaican planters first responded to abolitionist threats by increasing the enslaved population by a variety of means. Before 1808, they imported more Africans, but they could afford to be selective. After the abolition of the slave trade, planters throughout the British Caribbean shifted their attention to the problem of natural increase on their estates. Once the abolition of slavery moved from threat to reality, planter opinion shifted again, and planters eventually began to impress English and Christian values on their estates' enslaved children in an effort to socialize them into laborers who would be more manageable in the future. By 1833, there were no more options before them; they had no choice but to accept the inevitability of emancipation.

That year, Parliament passed a law that abolished slavery in all British dominions.[2] Rather than give immediate freedom to the slave community, however, parliamentarians created a six-year apprenticeship period "in order to fit you all for freedom."[3] Beginning on August 1, 1834, newly apprenticed slaves throughout the British Caribbean worked for wages and were housed, clothed, and fed by their estates. All children under the age of six were freed and became the complete responsibility of their parents. Special magistrates presided over the system and heard complaints from both slaves and planters as a means of ensuring fairness and a smooth transition. Although the law prohibited the flogging of females, Jamaica installed treadmills in each public workhouse or prison as the preferred form of punishment.[4] Last, England granted £20 million sterling as compensation to be divided among her colonies for the planters who filed by the deadline.[5] Skeptical that this system would work, many planters asked, "What is to become of the revenue of Jamaica?"[6]

Planters immediately attacked the problem by reorganizing and reinforcing the labor on their estates in an effort to extract as much labor as possible from their apprentices before the end of apprenticeship. All children six and older continued laboring in the fields and Great Houses from sunup to sundown. That way, "not an acre of land, not a sugar cane, not a labouring slave will be taken away from the owners."[7] Before apprenticeship natural decrease motivated planters to give children less laborious assignments with the hope that they would survive into adulthood and continue working on the estates. With full abolition on the horizon, however, many of these children would never enter the first gang in their adulthood. Consequently, overseers now had an incentive to work apprenticed children just as hard as adults, shortening their already brief childhood in the process.

The last vestiges of amelioration slipped away as female apprentices with six or more children returned to the fields. When Rebecca Stewart, a mother of nine on Chester Vale Estate in Port Royal, returned to the fields after a two-year hiatus, she lost her extra allowances of salt.[8] In St. James, Worcester Estate managers sent Mary and Diana Hall, who were previously exempt, back to the first gang, but Elenor Hall joined the second gang as she had an aged mother and six young children under her care.[9] Although some planters were more lenient in their placements of these women, the fact that women previously exempted from field labor returned to the fields shows the full extent of the changes in planter opinion toward childhood that took place with apprenticeship. Under slavery, labor exemptions motivated women to have more children and rewarded those women who were able to keep their children alive. Under apprenticeship, natural increase was no longer an issue. Planters did not want to offer any sort of incentive for fertility, and they certainly could not afford to reward it.

Reorganization efforts stretched to the estate hospitals as well, as planters tried to ensure the profitability of their estates. As many plantation hospitals stopped providing food for those receiving medical care, others downsized their staff in order to put more laborers in the fields.[10] Some hospitals closed entirely and became estate prisons.[11] Although these changes affected everyone on the estate, other modifications specifically affected pregnant women and children. Jamaican law no longer required physicians to provide medical care and attention to children not bound to the estates;[12] therefore, rather than waste medical supplies and treatment on children who would never benefit the estate, medical care disappeared for many children below the age of six. Prenatal care ended as well, sending a message to pregnant women as to how the birth of their child would be received.

Enslaved children working in the Great House or under the tutelage of tradesmen and skilled slaves, who enjoyed a higher standard of living under amelioration, joined the second or first gangs as field apprentices. In 1835, special magistrates conducted an inquest on the suicide of a cattleman on an estate in Jamaica. Since the passing of the apprenticeship laws, the cattleman's owner had reassigned the boys assisting him. As a result, the cattleman was unable to manage the cattle alone and was flogged by his overseer for negligence. Soon after, the cattleman committed suicide. Although his owner felt that he was putting the boys to better use in the fields, he now had to find an apprentice to manage the estate's cattle. As young domestics began cutting cane and picking coffee for the first time in their lives, children preparing for a life as tradesmen and skilled workers left their tools and livestock duties behind for more menial tasks in the fields. There they would be much more profitable.[13]

Although apprenticed children were not required to work the twelve-hour days they did as slaves, they were now responsible for their own food and water, because, in their labor reorganization efforts, planters discontinued the use of field cooks and water carriers. These former slaves joined the first and second gangs in the fields.[14] During amelioration, enslaved children were provided with extra food or special morning meals, but estate managers discontinued these extra allowances and expected apprenticed children to provide and cook their own food during their short lunch breaks. Some planters retaliated against the labor restrictions set in place by expecting their laborers to work without breaks for lunch and water. At Latium Estate in St. James, for example, the bookkeeper Benjamin M'Mahon witnessed a gang of young boys and girls from nine to twelve years of age working in the fields from "dawn of day till dark at night, without giving them time to eat a single meal; and this they were obliged to do in all weathers . . . returning at night, with cold and hunger."[15] Other planters allowed lunch breaks but restricted their apprentices from leaving the fields to get water when needed.[16]

As planters reorganized the labor, they habitually tried to convince workers to bind their free children as apprentices to their estates. Much to these planters' frustration, however, most apprentices refused. In October 1834, just two months after the apprenticeship system went into effect, planters desperately petitioned the Assembly "to oblige negro apprentices, who are parents of children under six years of age, to bind them as apprentices." But no amendment was made. Unable to accept that their apprentices preferred to support their children themselves rather than turn their children's care over to the estate, planters convinced themselves that there was a secret agency working against them. Although no one could provide proof, many planters pointed fingers at the clergymen ministering on their estates.[17]

A few planters tried to understand the motive behind their apprentices' refusal to bind their children to their estates. "I think it is only natural that they should wish them to remain as they are," planter William Tharpe said before the Jamaican Assembly in 1834.[18] Aside from protecting their children from a life of labor, apprentices fought for a negotiated freedom for their children. As they increasingly realized the importance their owners and overseers placed on the economic possibilities childhood presented to them, the island's former slaves understood that they held the upper hand in this situation. Not only did planters need children on their estates to ensure a labor force after apprenticeship, but they also needed parental permission in order to bind those children to their estates.

Meanwhile the Jamaican Assembly tried to appease their constituents with the passage of a bill in November 1834 allowing for the importation of field laborers and mechanics from Europe, although it did not duplicate the volume imported during the slave trade.[19] Archival sources do not indicate the exact number of European laborers brought into Jamaica during this time, but they do suggest that planters imported a significant number of children. In 1837 Cape Clear Estate in St. Mary had nine such indentured servants, six of them fifteen and younger, and on Belmore Castle in Trelawny a little over half of the forty-four mechanics and field laborers who recently arrived from Liverpool were children.[20] We do not know exactly how many indentured children came into Jamaica during the apprenticeship period, but their presence suggests that some planters still regarded children as an investment. By investing their money in more children than adults, the owners of Cape Clear Estate and Belmore Castle guaranteed themselves laborers well acclimated to field labor in their adulthood.

As planters lamented the economic and political pressures of the new labor restrictions, only nine children below the age of six became apprentices between 1834 and 1838.[21] According to a circular commissioned by King's House in Spanishtown, St. Catherine in July 1838, five-and-a-half-year-old Isabella Malcolm, five-year-old John Malcolm, and their two-year-old sister Molly became the apprentices of Margaret Gilzean, owner of Pedro Estate in Hanover, in September 1836.[22] Since Molly was far too young to work, her status as an apprentice gave her the support she needed without putting her in the fields; Isabella and Malcolm would join the children's gang sometime in 1837. Although archival sources give no indication of the motive behind their apprenticeship, it is possible that their mother was unable to support them and believed it was in their best interest to be bound to the estate, which would require only three years of minimal work in the children's gang. Or she may have preferred to apprentice them rather than do the extra work she would have to perform for their support. Whatever the motive, Isabella and Malcolm worked for only one year before gaining their freedom in 1838.

Apprenticeship complicated the nature of childhood as it existed on the island. Under slavery children rapidly shifted from childhood to adulthood when they left the plantation nurseries for the fields. Once children under the age of six became free in 1834, however, their childhood had an opportunity to continue without planter interference. These children would no longer grow to be laborers, tradesmen, or breeding wenches and were no longer born into a state of slavery. For those children between the ages of six and fifteen, however, their childhood suffered even more under apprenticeship. Thrust into an accelerated adulthood in terms of labor expectations, these children were expected to work even harder than they did as slaves. As a result the nature of childhood in Jamaica became age-specific: under the age of six children gained the freedom to be children; between the ages of six and fifteen they abruptly became adults.

Therefore, children under six suddenly became worthless to planters, signifying only lost future laborers. Furthermore, any natural increase of the African Jamaican population was of no benefit to Jamaican planters, because all children born on or after August 1, 1834, were free at birth.[23] As older slaves died, a new generation of laborers would not be there to replace them. Suddenly, the struggle against infant and child mortality and low fertility was a moot issue. What became a serious issue, however, was the presence of these free children on Jamaica's estates.

The Struggle

It was no secret that many planters felt their apprentices overindulged the free children on their estates. The Jamaican missionary Hope Masterton Waddell noted that some apprentices regarded their children as the "King's free children," considering them to be superior in status, above work, and beyond punishment. Consequently, many planters argued that their slave villages were overrun with idle children, whose freedom turned them into lazy and troublesome vagrants.[24] As they worked to extract as much labor as possible from the children and adults apprenticed to their estates, these free children became a threat to the civil and political economy of the island. Persuading parents to bind their children to the estates was proving to be unsuccessful, and planters began to view these children as a threat to their very livelihoods.

Since English law prohibited Jamaican planters from apprenticing free children to their estates without their mother's permission, free children lived "in a certain degree at the expense of the estate."[25] On Bounty Hall Estate in St. James, for example, bookkeepers reported in 1837 that the estate financially supported 134 free children at a rate of 5 pounds colonial currency per annum.[26] Jamaican law, however, did not require planters to feed, clothe, or house these free children.[27] If parents were unable to feed or clothe them, "they became dependent on their old masters, they would come under the law of the apprenticeship, and have to work out their time."[28] In other words, any free children who did not receive sufficient food and clothing from their parents could become indentured laborers until their twenty-first birthday.[29] Although apprenticeship was scheduled to last for a period of six years, the law said nothing about indentured servitude. As young white indentured laborers from England and Europe began joining Jamaican apprentices in the fields, parents realized that while the apprenticeship of these children may have been illegal, their indentureship was perfectly legal.

As a means of protecting their free children from this economic loophole, some parents moved them off the estate and away from planter influence. On John Salmon's Jamaican properties, for example, "the greater part . . . are off the property staying here and there with their friends as the parents say."[30] Some planters too considered this option. When John W. Cooper inspected Simon Taylor's properties in the parish of St. Thomas in the East in 1835, he suggested that Burrowfield Pen send the majority of the holding's free children to neighboring Lysson's Estate as "much alteration is required here if it is decided to continue in its present state." Cooper reported that the pen's apprentices were "very mismanaged"; on a small pen like Burrowfield, overseers needed every hand working in the fields in order to maintain their pre-apprenticeship profits. Free children drained the pen's resources, but an estate the size of Lysson's could afford to support the children better than Burrowfield, though they would still be a burden. Cooper merely tried to alleviate that burden somewhat by delegating responsibility from a small, struggling pen to another, more profitable estate.[31]

Some female apprentices went so far as to state that they would rather see their children dead than apprentice them to their estate.[32] Other laborers refused to apprentice their children out of mistrust. In their inspections of the apprentices on several Jamaican estates in 1838, Thomas A. Thome and Horace Kimball reported that no laborer was under the age of six: "None of them will work for hire, or in any way put themselves under [the manager's] control, as the parents fear there is some plot laid for making them apprentices, and through that process reducing them to slavery."[33]

Many planters tried to use the situation to their advantage. Under apprenticeship, Parliament limited the time Jamaica's laborers spent in the fields to forty hours per week at a maximum of nine hours per day.[34] Because this was a significant reduction from the twelve hours a day slaves averaged, Jamaican planters felt the pressure of falling profits. Fewer hours in the fields yielded smaller sugar and coffee shipments, and planters feared an apprenticeship-induced bankruptcy. Estate managers and overseers attacked these restrictions by creating a barter system that offered conditional support to free children on the estate. On Lysson's

Estate managers sustained clothing and food allowances for the estate's free children so long as their parents supplied "an equivalent portion of extra labor."[35] Other estates offered their laborers the same option, hoping that the extra labor would raise their profits. Planter Thomas McCornack happily reported to the Jamaican Assembly in 1834 that his slaves worked forty-five hours each week instead of forty, and George Gordon's apprentices continued working the same hours they did as slaves during harvest.[36]

Other planters offered medical care to free children in an effort to entice their parents to work extra hours. Using expensive medical supplies on children who would never work on the estate was simply a waste of money, but the extra labor was a way to justify the expense and contributed to the estate's profitability. On Rio Magno Estate in St. Catherine, for example, the former slaves of the estate worked together to ensure medical care for every free child by beginning work an hour earlier each day.[37] Other planters could not justify the expense. On Llanrumney Estate in St. Mary, planters provided herring and cloth to the free children but barred them from the plantation hospital no matter how long their parents labored in the fields.[38]

Although it is difficult to measure the value the slaves placed on their children before apprenticeship, their willingness to work extra hours without pay adds insight. As the entire labor force on Rio Magno Estate banded together to protect the children of the estate from sickness and death, their actions illustrate the importance that the apprentice community placed on freedom and childhood. Under slavery, enslaved Jamaicans knew that their children faced a life of hard labor and harsh punishment and would grow up to be slaves. These children were the first generation to experience freedom, and that freedom gave them the opportunity to live as children rather than chattel. Working extra hours ensured that these children received the food and care they needed in order to experience that future to its fullest. Understanding this, planters reassigned the value they placed on free children from burden to bargaining chip. If planters could not use these children as apprentices, they would use them as an incentive to increase the productivity of those apprentices already working in the fields.

Pregnancy posed another problem to the economic viability of the labor force. As if apprenticeship turned back the hands of time, planters once again believed that pregnancy reduced productivity on Jamaican estates. Pregnancy slowed workers or kept them out of the fields altogether after bouts of morning sickness or miscarriage. Although there is no evidence that planters tried to discourage their female apprentices from becoming pregnant, natural increase was no longer profitable. Once again, planters felt it more rational to use their female laborers to their full potential in the fields, only this time the women were not easily replaceable commodities as they were before the abolition of the slave trade.

Prenatal care also disappeared under apprenticeship. Sukey Morris, an apprentice on Newman Hall in St. James, issued a complaint before the special magistrate against her plantation manager, Mr. Wilson, in January 1836. Six months pregnant and unable to perform the labor required of the first gang, was punished with solitary confinement overnight and was fed only two plantains. On her release, she resumed her work in the first gang tying canes. Special Magistrate Carnaby ordered Wilson to pay a fine of 1 pound colonial currency. This meager fine revealed Carnaby's disapproval of Wilson's treatment of Sukey, and her return to the first gang suggests bias against her unborn child. As a slave, Sukey would have moved into the second or children's gang on the estate, where the lighter work protected both her and her unborn child from the stresses of harsh field labor. As an apprentice, her pregnancy became a burden, and her free child was of no use to the estate. Furthermore, Sukey's pregnancy slowed down her work, and she was unable to tie canes as fast as the other slaves.[39]

Elizabeth Nimble on Resource Estate in Port Royal continued working into her eighth month of pregnancy. Now that Resource Estate's slaves were apprentices and their unborn children were burdens, "Busha make woman with Child work in the field till they deliver along with the Great Gang and two weeks after delivery make them turn out to the field."[40] Eliza Smith, an apprentice on Mount Pleasant Estate in St. Elizabeth, had a similar experience. While working alongside the first gang in August 1834, Eliza gave birth to a stillborn child in her seventh month of pregnancy. Instead of receiving the customary month off from labor after giving birth, Eliza returned to the fields in just two short weeks. In an angry letter to Eliza's owner, Robert McDaniel, Special Magistrate William Oldrey wrote, "You have worked the woman to the last moment, and after giving birth to a seven month's child, to turn her out in less than a fortnight to work, proves the cruelty of her case."[41] Eliza's complaint sparked an inspection of the property as well as the condition of the apprentices, but Oldrey does not indicate whether McDaniel received a fine.

Other overseers severely punished pregnant women if their work was slow. In 1835, when Sarah Murdoch's morning sickness affected her field duties on London Ridge Estate, she was punished with fourteen days of hard labor and time on the treadmill. On her fourth day in the workhouse, she prematurely gave birth to a stillborn child. Unable to find someone to bury the child, Sarah performed the burial herself on the workhouse grounds. Although an extreme case, her experiences show the complete disregard of the white community for her unborn child. Under slavery workhouse administrators would have buried the child at the expense of Sarah's owners. That was now Sarah's responsibility.[42]

As planters expected all female apprentices to work to their full capacity and beyond in the fields, many women "might be refused, and often were" denied access to nurses and child care.[43] With the closings of plantation nurseries on many Jamaican estates, special magistrates discovered "the intemperate conduct of the overseers" who refused their female apprentices the necessary time to breastfeed their children.[44] Apprentice James Williams remembered one overseer who "say the children free, and the law don't allow no time to take care of them; it is only the good will of the driver that ever let woman suckle the children."[45] Some planters compromised by allowing their female apprentices to take turns wet-nursing all of the children at once.[46] Others expected nursing mothers to make other arrangements for their infants, as "they do not do one third of the work of the others." Some women, like the enslaved women on Rio Magno Estate, received a few extra hours in the morning to attend to their children before coming to the fields.[47] If some women left the fields during the day to feed their children, as did Margaret McDonald of Berwick Estate in St. George, they were punished.[48] As planters forced their female apprentices to work as much as possible, they reinforced the idea that the free children on their estates were only a burden.

Many women simply tied their children to their back as they did before the creation of plantation nurseries, but some planters refused them even this. When Ann Johnstone, an apprentice on Recess Plantation in St. Thomas in the Vale, came to the fields one morning with her eleven-month-old tied to her back, estate manager Mr. Gyles ordered her to take the child home. Ann refused, stating that there was no one in her hut to mind the child. Gyles then ordered her to turn her baby over to an old woman named Lettice. Objecting to the responsibility, Lettice informed both Gyles and Ann that she was not able to mind herself, let alone an eleven-month-old child. Frustrated, Gyles told Lettice "if [she] would not mind the child, she might throw it in the pasture." Gyles then ordered the driver to take Ann's baby to Lettice if she returned to the field with the child strapped to her back. Despite her orders, Ann returned to the field with her child, who was immediately taken to Lettice. Lettice refused to mind the baby and put it in the pasture, where it stayed until nightfall. That evening, Ann collected her child and returned to the fields the next day with her child again tied to her back. This time Ann was allowed to keep her child with her. Although it is not known whether the driver overlooked the child or Gyles thought it best not to push the issue any further, Ann continued to work in the fields with her child tied to her back.[49]

Other women took a more organized approach to their resistance. In 1837, one year before apprenticeship ended on the island, ten women on Lansquinet Estate in the parish of St. Ann refused to take their children into the fields with them as long as it was raining. Staying in their huts until the rain stopped, the women went to the fields after breakfast with their children in tow. Although Lansquinet managers allowed mothers to work with their children tied to their back, their tardiness guaranteed them an appearance before Special Magistrate Pryce. Unlike his more sympathetic peers, Pryce sentenced the ten women to work six Saturdays of extra labor in the fields. They refused, stating that their provision grounds were more than six miles away, and since Lansquinet managers deprived them of their additional salt-fish allowance, they needed that time to work their grounds for extra provisions. Incensed by their audacity, Pryce sent the women to the St. Ann Workhouse, where they worked in chains and wore iron collars in the penal gang with their children tied to their back. On their return to Lansquinet, Pryce ordered "a strong body of police be sent on the estate, where 'a barrack was prepared for them' to quell, we presume . . . a rebellion among the nursing mothers."[50]

We do not know whether the women on Lansquinet succeeded in obtaining the goals of their resistance, but women throughout the island significantly affected the workings of their estates. Just two months after apprenticeship began in Jamaica, many planters feared sugar production in the parish of St. James would end if the women's acts of passive resistance were not stopped.[51] One year later, in March 1835, Governor Sligo received a report from Special Magistrate J. Kennet Dawson concerning the district of Manchioneal in the parish of St. Thomas in the East. According to Dawson, "the conduct of the women retards greatly the well-doing of the estates, being extremely turbulent, obstinate, and insolent."[52] Other women threatened the bookkeepers and estate managers, whom they blamed for the changes taking place on their estates. On Albany Estate in Westmoreland managers summoned the police in August 1834 to reason with the female apprentices, who "wanted to commit murder . . . on the bookkeeper."[53]

Although apprenticeship gave freedom to their children, female apprentices in Jamaica clearly resented the actions of those in authority on their estates. These women, who once felt pressure and coercion from above to have more children, now saw the disregard their owners and overseers had for the lives they created. While some women agreed to work extra hours for the care and support of their children, others refused to allow the system to attach a price to the freedom of their children. As planters made it clear that free children were unwanted on their estates, the actions of their female apprentices showed their owners that they valued their children's freedom above anything in the world.

Apprenticeship's Lasting Effect

Realizing that the free children on their estates would not be of use to the country's economic profitability during the apprenticeship period, Jamaican planters intensified their efforts at child socialization in order to make these children useful after this period ended. As early as 1810, planters responded to threats against slavery by educating enslaved children for their roles as free workers. An island that was once opposed to the religious conversion of the enslaved population reluctantly accepted missionaries of all denominations in the hope that they would help make enslaved children loyal and controllable commodities. Once English abolitionists succeeded in their fight against slavery and Jamaican planters found themselves supporting the free children on their plantations, estate managers and bookkeepers once again enlisted the clergy's help. Many in the white community were of the opinion that apprentices "took too much care of their children, going to the extreme of over indulgence."[54] As a result, free children "are bred up in absolute idleness."[55] Planters found some comfort in the fact that they still had the next six years to mold and influence the children on their estates.

Echoing sentiments that "increased knowledge and civilization [could] enlarge their ideas, improve their morals and manners . . . and render them good subjects and fellow citizens admitted to respectability of character," Parliament extended Jamaica the funds necessary to increase educational efforts of the island's children.[56] Parliament allocated £25,000 sterling for education in the colonies, with more promised when needed, and Jamaica built more schools and applied to London for more instructors.[57] Meanwhile, parish vestries came forward with petitions calling for increased legislation and financial assistance to support the increased education efforts. The parish vestry in Portland, for example, was alarmed "at the portentious aspect which the affecting state of these children bear on the future well-being of the island; no longer subject to the commands of their former masters . . . free from every controlling power." The Westmoreland vestry argued that the future cultivation of the island depended mainly on "the increased civilization" of these children.[58] Convinced that the religious socialization and basic education of Jamaica's free children were key factors to ensure the smooth transition from apprenticeship to full emancipation, planters intensified their efforts at socially conditioning the children of the island.

This time, however, planters did not use religious education as a means of increasing the number of children on their estates. Whereas missionaries saw this as an opportunity to reach the souls they could not reach under slavery, planters realized the opportunity enlightened children presented after apprenticeship. Continuing to impress ideas of morality, honor, and loyalty, the clergy could link ideas of "disgrace and irreligion to the disobedient and the sluggard."[59] In other words, religious education could be used to enforce the idea that idleness was a sin. Blaming parental overindulgence and immoral influence for this idleness, planters felt that it was more important than ever to remove free children from their parents' control. Meanwhile, as missionaries and teachers impressed English customs and beliefs on their young students, the educational curriculum continued to demand the performance of small tasks around the estates, such as on Hopeton and Lenox Estates.[60] Educating free children not only ensured a more controllable and "civilized" population after emancipation, but it created a loophole to the apprenticeship laws. Education enabled planters to put free children to use on the estate performing duties that more able-bodied apprentices need not perform. Although free children were still a burden to the estate, their presence there was a little more justified than before. And since the majority of the children being educated on the island were free, planters assigned less importance to the education of children between the ages of six and fifteen. Planters clearly expected these children to work in the same capacity as the adults on their estates; in fact, after 1834, some planters considered these children to be adults.

To ensure that more free children entered the schools, planters offered their apprentices various incentives. Jamaican proprietor William Miller offered to pay his apprentices for any extra time they worked if they placed their children in school.[61] Others favored educating their child apprentices, but only if the work did not suffer. Estate manager John

Salmon suggested that employer James George Crabbe create a schedule on his estates by which "so many hours daily [would] be given to instruction & so many to labor" to guarantee that the children still worked in the fields but received the education they needed.[62] Just as they did with food and medical care, Jamaican planters used education as a bargaining chip with their apprentices.

The largest incentive, however, was the care and support that these children received while they were in school. For parents who could not support their children as well as they had under slavery, education was a viable solution to the problem of child care. Because apprentices worked extra hours in the fields, many could not find the time to work their provision grounds, make clothing, and take care of their children. Furthermore, plantation nurseries ceased to exist. Although some women brought their children to the fields with them, they were punished if their work was slow or they attended their children instead of working. Other women knew bringing their children with them to the fields would result in severe punishment. Schools served as a surrogate nursery of sorts, creating a suitable environment where women could place their children and still fulfill their labor and household duties.

As public opinion pushed for the education of Jamaica's free children, the legislature felt pressure from Governor Sligo to make education more accessible. When the Jamaican Assembly complained about the inadequacy of education on the island to the House of Commons in 1836, Governor Sligo angrily responded in a speech before the Jamaican Assembly that same year that they "have taken no steps to make it available."[63] Unless the children received an education, Jamaica's apprentices would continue to raise their children in idleness.

A year later, at the behest of the House of Commons, C. J. Latrobe began investigating the state of education on the island. After attending and inspecting each school on the island and detailing the number of students, administration costs, and the amount of government aid each school received, Latrobe offered a detailed report on the many difficulties Jamaican planters faced in building schools, motivating the slaves, and providing educators throughout the island's parishes. According to Latrobe, planters had trouble finding land and workers to build schools in both rural and urban areas. Not only did the island experience a shortage of artisans and skilled laborers after apprenticeship, but the majority of Jamaica's land was used for sugar and coffee. Planters were reluctant to sacrifice crops to build schools during this time of falling profits. Furthermore, despite islandwide efforts to educate more children, Latrobe noted a lack of organization on the part of missionaries and the Jamaican Assembly to make education more accessible. Although parish and church schools remained open after apprenticeship began, "there exists a great diversity of opinion in the island as to the probable success that many attend" the estate and plantation schools of the island. Three-quarters of those in attendance were the free children of apprentices. Child apprentices attended in low numbers and received "the scantiest proportion of instruction," either because of a lack of encouragement or because of a lack of time; education was not a priority for these children, who were expected to work in the fields in the same capacity as the adults. Therefore, Jamaica's free children received the most benefit from the island's schools.[64]

Despite the problems outlined by Latrobe, the number of free children in Jamaican schools grew. In 1834 only 8,321 free children attended school; four years later Jamaican planters reported that 38,754 of the 38,899 free children on the island were in school.[65] Apprenticeship, then, created a sharp increase in the education of plantation children. Although enslaved women tried to keep their children away from English influence, the apprenticeship system forced the women to place their children in school, where they received the care and support they needed. As a result, free children progressed through their childhood in an environment that became increasingly more English. While apprenticeship freed children below the age of six, it established an environment that enabled the continuation of the outside influence and manipulation that challenged the stability of those beliefs and traditions these children retained from their parents and kinship groups as slaves. Jamaican children grew to adulthood influenced by both English and African cultural traditions and beliefs. What developed was the beginnings of a uniquely Jamaican cultural identity.

Summary

James Mursell Phillippo wrote in his contemporary history of Jamaica, "It is unreasonable to suppose that the faults of years were to be eradicated in a day."[66] Freedom was given, but it was a conditional freedom. As apprenticeship changed the nature of childhood in Jamaica, children shifted from investment to liability overnight. Yet, just as planters devalued the children on their estates, the abolition of slavery in Jamaica enables us to see the value the former slave community placed on these children as they demanded and often received a negotiated freedom for their children during this transitional period.

Ultimately, apprenticeship created a paradox of sorts in Jamaican slave society as it attached its own value to childhood and child worth. Although Parliament granted freedom to children below the age of six, it made no provision for their care and support. Meanwhile, as children changed from investments to burdens overnight, they became useful as bargaining chips for the planters, who feared economic ruin. Although the nature of slavery had always been exploitative in Jamaica, ameliorative policies disappeared as planters desperately tried to secure the profitability of their vulnerable estates. Consequently, the standard of living on Jamaica's plantations deteriorated to early eighteenth-century standards as planters desperately tried to protect their estates from economic ruin. Jamaican children faced the prospect of an undefined childhood after apprenticeship, one that was free from planter control and gave laborers as a whole hope for the future.

Despite the changes taking place in the world around them, Jamaica's apprentices demanded and often received a negotiated freedom for their children. As they worked to protect their children from a system that continued to exploit them by assigning conditions to their freedom, the value of childhood in the apprenticed community became clearly defined. This new generation of children had the opportunity to experience a childhood outside of slavery. Suddenly planters differentiated between children under six who were the responsibility of their parents and older children who were still part of the labor regime. Under this new system of apprenticeship, children between six and fifteen were thrust immediately into a premature adulthood, more than they were under slavery. Since planters had apprenticed labor on their estates for such a short period of time, this motivated them to push more children into the fields and work them harder. As these children entered adulthood at an even earlier age than before, free children became the only "real" children in Jamaica. To this end the apprenticeship system equated childhood with freedom, but it also set a powerful precedent for the civil status of emancipated African Jamaicans after 1840. With emancipation African Jamaicans began to claim control of their future. Therefore, apprenticeship laid the foundation for the shift in power that would take place in Jamaica's postemancipation economy.

Conclusions

Every moment of change has a catalyst. Throughout my discussion of the changing nature of childhood in Jamaica, the English abolitionist movement has been the main spark for that change. Prior to the ameliorative laws of 1788, enslaved children were nothing but a financial burden to the Jamaican plantation economy; they experienced extremely high mortality rates, and many died soon after birth. Beginning in 1783, when English abolitionists sent their first petition to Parliament calling for the abolition of the Atlantic slave trade, Jamaican enslaved children gradually shifted from burden to investment. As this transformation in planter opinion took shape, the role of the children as a viable economic commodity evolved by 1815 into a social investment as well, nearly a decade after English abolitionists succeeded in ending the slave trade and began focusing on the institution of slavery itself. Abolitionism sparked one last change in planter opinion, in 1834, when Parliament decreed the end of slavery after a short apprenticeship period. Under apprenticeship, children younger than six became financial burdens, while those between six and fifteen traveled toward adulthood even faster than they did as slaves. In one last effort to fight the abolition of slavery in Jamaica, planters and estate managers tried to make the best of their situation by using children as bargaining chips during this period.

What this reveals is a link between the changing nature of childhood, the changing nature of slavery, and the growth, influence, and impact of the British abolitionist movement. Planters, parliamentarians, and assemblymen all modified their definitions of value, risk, and investment as abolitionist sentiment gained support in England. As the abolitionist movement gained speed, it forced a reevaluation of the economic viability of enslaved children. Suddenly the planter elite began to wonder: Could children lead Jamaica's plantations to economic profitability and stability? While hindsight tells us that the logical answer is a resounding no, the planters were depending on enslaved children as a means of combating the economic devastation foreshadowed by the growing influence of British abolitionists.

Shifts in planter opinion toward slave childhood became more apparent as abolitionist sentiment slowly changed the nature of slavery during the late eighteenth century, when planters hoped to raise enslaved children to adulthood and delay the economic ruin they so feared. The children became extremely valuable to Jamaica's plantations and estates as planters began to understand a need for change in the management and treatment of the women and children on their estates. Definitions of risk ceased to include enslaved children, as Jamaican planters and estate managers had no choice but to focus their attention on the natural increase of their slaves. The Jamaican Assembly passed legislative measures ameliorating the condition of the enslaved population in an effort to create an environment conducive to natural increase.

Once abolitionists focused on ending slavery in the British colonies not long after their success at abolishing the Atlantic slave trade, the nature of slavery changed again. As a result the nature of childhood changed as well as planters accepted the inevitability of abolition. They began to focus on the Christian education of the enslaved children on their estates, now seeing the children as a social investment. The identity of these children shifted from slave to future freedman, and their education began to define freedom for the slave community, as much as their owners would allow. By the 1820s, enslaved children had become a top priority for many on the island.

Despite this rise in children's importance, these changes in the nature of childhood occurred purely out of economic need. Although planter ideas of child worth changed during this period, planter ideas of childhood as they related to the enslaved population really did not. Jamaican planters felt no humanitarian pull toward improving the quality of life for the children on their estates. If they did, they would have continued their ameliorative policies during apprenticeship. Instead, planters and estate managers instantly abandoned these policies for more oppressive measures that extracted as much labor as possible from their former slaves. As a result, the standard of living on Jamaica's plantations deteriorated to early eighteenth-century standards. Free children became financial burdens overnight, and their childhood became useful only as a bargaining chip for extracting more labor from their parents. Children between the ages of six and fifteen suffered an even shorter childhood than they did as slaves, as planters and estate managers found an incentive in working these children as hard as the adults. With few exceptions, planter ideas of childhood in Jamaica throughout this period existed purely in economic terms.

However, race complicated planter ideas of childhood and slavery. As the mulatto community grew within the slave villages, skin color separated mulatto children from the remainder of the enslaved population and enabled many of these children to enjoy a higher standard of living. At the same time, however, Jamaican planters and estate managers perceived their whiteness as a defect in their potential as future field laborers, devaluing their worth as an economic investment as laborers and potential breeders. As a result, children of color remained financial burdens to the plantation economy. Further complicating matters was their connection to the white community, as that connection sparked recognition and differentiation between chattel and child. White fathers increasingly manumitted and provided for their children, and this acceptance drove the Jamaican Assembly to enact restrictive measures on the amount of money and property mulatto children could inherit from their white fathers. As more fathers and relatives accepted mulatto children, the Jamaican Assembly tightened their restrictive measures. By 1813, however, the Assembly lightened the restrictions, allowing the mulatto community to increase their standing within Jamaican society. Although mulatto children did not achieve equality, the white community increasingly acknowledged the mulatto children of the island as being different from the chattel that labored on their estates.

As European society began to recognize the various stages of childhood taking place among white children, the changing nature of slavery within the Jamaican plantation complex prompted planters to recognize several stages of childhood among enslaved children.[1] These stages, however, differed from those envisioned in Europe as well as those defined by the Jamaican slave community. Under slavery and apprenticeship, the various stages of slave childhood revolved around plantation labor and economic need. Infants and children did not work on the estate, but boys and girls labored in the third and second gangs. Before 1816, boyhood and girlhood began around age five and ended within ten years as entrance into the first gang signified the beginning of adulthood. After

1816, when the Jamaican Assembly passed a law prohibiting the rape of enslaved girls under ten, childhood extended to age ten. Boyhood and girlhood, then, existed between the ages of eleven and fifteen.

As we have seen, however, Jamaican planters and estate managers added new stages to slave childhood as the abolitionist movement intensified in England. The titles *man-boy* and *woman-girl* increasingly included fourteen- and fifteen-year-olds just on the cusp of puberty, further proof of a link between the changing natures of childhood and slavery. As youth became a more desirable characteristic of slave imports to Jamaica and "breeding wenches" and "belly-women" increased in number on the island's estates, planters and traders frequently attached these labels to children under sixteen. As a result, some planters referred to girls as young as thirteen as women-girls.

These shifting definitions of childhood were subjective as well. Some planters categorized enslaved children between the ages of five and eight working in the third gang as boys and girls but classified the gang in which they worked as the children's gang. Interestingly, those same planters categorized all enslaved children not working on the estate as children. Other planters classified all enslaved children not working on the estate as infants, while the children worked in the children's or third gang and the boys and girls worked in the second gang. Furthermore, planters often contradicted themselves where children were concerned. Although Jamaican planters and estate managers did not consider the girls and women-girls who worked in the second gang as adults, some took these girls as sexual partners. Despite an acknowledgment of their sexuality and their entrance into adult situations, these girls remained girls until they joined the first gang as adults at the age of sixteen.

As the nature of slavery and childhood changed, enslaved children struggled to survive and identify with the world around them. For Jamaican planters, childhood was an economic investment; for Jamaican enslaved children, childhood was a rushed and contested process filled with immense poverty, hard labor, familial separation, and death. Although the development of ameliorative policies promised them an improved standard of living after 1788, these policies did not promise a childhood free from planter interference and manipulation. Watching their parents toil in the fields, suffer under the lash, and fend off sexual assault instilled in them an idea of their future as chattel. When these children left the plantation nurseries for the fields, they immediately began the shift from childhood to adulthood. Forced into adulthood before their time, Jamaican enslaved children would never escape the traumas they faced on a daily basis. As they moved from gang to gang, they attempted to negotiate their place within the plantation complex through acts of violence, theft, self-destruction, and even murder. By the time these children reached the second gang, the tasks they performed alongside the first gang quickly accelerated their entrance into adulthood. As planters increasingly acknowledged that enslaved children could grow up to be productive adults, boys quickly matured into laborers and tradesmen while girls became breeding wenches and eventually belly-women, their short childhood over almost as soon as it began.

How these children perceived themselves is more difficult to discern. While their acts of violence and disobedience suggest how some related to their situation and the situation of those around them, their voices remain silent. Some children identified with their parents' shipmates as family or kin; others became part of an adopted family or kinship group. Some parents encouraged their mulatto children to reject their West African heritage in an attempt to assimilate into English society, while other parents raised their children the way they themselves were raised. These children may have identified themselves as eboe and coromontee, African, colored, or simply Creole.

Although some West African cultural practices and beliefs—such as naming practices, folklore traditions, and language—were transferred to Jamaican enslaved children, what these children retained and passed on to their own children is unknown. We may never know how Jamaican enslaved children identified with the diverse cultural landscape of the island during our period of study. Despite moderate planter interference and manipulation, we do know that slave parents had many opportunities to raise their children on their own terms. By 1815, when abolitionist threats against the institution of slavery intensified, slave parents struggled to maintain control over that process as planters attempted to change the nature of African cultural identity in Jamaica by impressing Christian and English values on enslaved children on their estates. This educational conditioning complicates things, as planters and estate managers increasingly spoke of their success in Christianizing enslaved children rather than the peculiar beliefs and practices of the slaves on their estates. Therefore, our only window into the slave point of view becomes more and more biased as planters, estate managers, and missionaries intensified their efforts at creating a more loyal and easily controllable generation of slaves. One thing is sure, however: Christian education challenged the traditions and beliefs practiced within the slave villages.

As Jamaican planters and estate managers strengthened their education efforts under apprenticeship, Christian education continued to challenge these traditions and beliefs. Apprenticeship freed children under six and created an opportunity for the sharp increase in the education of plantation children. Enslaved women struggled to keep their children away from English influence and to protect them from racist policies, but the apprenticeship system forced them to place their free children in school, where they received the care and support they needed. These children grew to adulthood influenced by both English and West African cultural traditions and beliefs, aiding in the creation of a Jamaican cultural identity. Although archival sources shift their focus to the Christianization efforts of the white community after 1815, we do get a sense of how the slave community as a whole envisioned childhood during this point in time. More important, we see how the slave community valued childhood. As whites voiced their dissatisfaction with their slaves' unwillingness to educate their children in the ways of English morals and culture, ideas of freedom as they related to enslaved children began to surface during the last decade of slavery. As the role of enslaved children shifted from slave to future freedman, the education of these children inspired a realistic definition of freedom for slaves for the first time in their lives. Sparked by the abolitionist movement, this definition developed further after 1834, as mothers succeeded in negotiating and securing the conditional freedom of their children under apprenticeship by working extra hours in the fields. Although planter opinion once again perceived children as burdens, their ability to use free children as bargaining chips actually enabled these burgeoning ideas of freedom to develop further during this period. Whereas Jamaican planters and estate managers no longer relied on the free children on their estates, the freedom of children under apprenticeship gave Jamaica's laborers hope for the future, a future when children would have the possibility of a childhood and the power to define themselves. In the end, childhood became synonymous with freedom.

Notes

Introduction

1. Trelawny, *An Essay Concerning Slavery*, 4–6. Although Trelawny published his essay anonymously, not everyone is quick to give him credit. While Peter C. Hogg and George Boulukos attribute the essay to Trelawny, James Robertson prefers to keep the essay's author anonymous. See *The African Slave Trade and Its Suppression*, 140; Boulukos, *The Grateful Slave*, 4–7, 8, 10, 13; Robertson, "An Essay Concerning Slavery."

2. Higman, *Plantation Jamaica*, 1.

3. Burnard, *Mastery, Tyranny, and Desire*, 13; O'Shaughnessy, *An Empire Divided*, xi–xii; *The Oxford History of the British Empire*, 584.

4. Hall, *Civilising Subjects*, 83.

5. Burnard, *Mastery, Tyranny, and Desire*, 14.

6. Ibid.

7. Higman, *Plantation Jamaica*, 1; Higman, *Jamaica Surveyed*, 8.

8. Petley, *Slaveholders in Jamaica*, 6.

9. Burnard, *Mastery, Tyranny, and Desire*, 14; Burnard, "'Prodigious Riches,'" 517. To be fair, Jamaica's economy was not without its challenges. Frequent wars, the American Revolution, devastating hurricanes, and declining sugar prices all tested the island. Jamaican planters hit their peak in 1805 with that year's sugar export, and like most planters living in the Caribbean during this period, they experienced increasing economic decline up to the emancipation of slavery in 1834. For more on Jamaica's economy during this period, see Sheridan, "The Wealth of Jamaica in the Eighteenth Century"; Higman, *Slave Population and Economy*; Coclanis, "The Wealth of British America"; Higman, "The Internal Economy of Jamaican Pens"; Burnard, "The Curious Decline of Jamaican Sugar Planters."

10. Higman, *Plantation Jamaica*, 2; Burnard, *Mastery, Tyranny, and Desire*, 14.

11. Brown, *The Reaper's Garden*, 2.

12. Burnard, *Mastery, Tyranny, and Desire*, 17; Burnard, "'Prodigious Riches,'" 506.

For more on white mortality in Jamaica, see Burnard, "A Failed Settler Society"; Burnard, "European Migration to Jamaica"; Burnard, "'The Countrie Continues Sicklie.'"

13. Petley, *Slaveholders in Jamaica*, 2. Created in 1718, the Deficiency Acts imposed fines on planters who failed to have the required proportion of whites to slaves on their property. Absentee planters were required to have one white resident for every twenty-four slaves, while resident planters were required to have one white resident for every thirty slaves. In 1734, the rate was increased to one white resident for every twenty slaves for absentee planters. See Higman, *Plantation Jamaica*, 22. For more on absenteeism in Jamaica, see Hall, "Absentee-Proprietorship in the British West Indies"; Hall, "Some Aspects of the 'Deficiency' Question"; Burnard, "Passengers Only"; Higman, *Plantation Jamaica*, 22–29.

14. See Hall, *Civilising Subjects*, 72; Roberts, *Slavery and the Enlightenment*, 15. Interestingly, Bryan Edwards argues that the island imported a total of 610,000 Africans between 1700 and 1786 alone (*The History, Civil and Commercial, of the British Colonies*, 55). Philip Curtin set the number of total imports to the island, not counting those Africans sold to parties outside of Jamaica, at 747,500 (*The Atlantic Slave Trade*, 53).

15. Burnard, *Mastery, Tyranny, and Desire*, 15; Roberts, *Slavery and the Enlightenment*, 15. Although the Act for the Abolition of the Slave Trade received royal assent in May 1807, slavers had until March 1, 1808, to comply. According to the Trans-Atlantic Slave Trade Database, a total of 3,561 voyages list Jamaica as their principal port of disembarkation from 1655 to 1808, estimating that 927,160 Africans were imported to the island during those years. The database does not indicate how many of those Africans stayed in Jamaica or were sold elsewhere (Eltis, *Voyages*).

16. Burnard, *Mastery, Tyranny, and Desire*, 15; Petley, *Slaveholders in Jamaica*, 2. Philip Curtin argues that Jamaica purchased only 1/5 of the slaves transported across the Atlantic (*The Atlantic Slave Trade*, 9).

17. Roberts, *Slavery and the Enlightenment*, 14.

18. *Poverty and Life Expectancy*, 25. While most historians agree that Africans imported to labor on Caribbean sugar plantations lived an average of seven years, Trevor Burnard makes an interesting assertion that whites suffered much higher mortality rates than the Africans and Creoles on the island, despite the fact Jamaica's enslaved Africans suffered from malnutrition, hard labor, and harsh punishment. As previously mentioned, Burnard argues that European immigrants to the island could expect to live no more than twelve years after their arrival, suggesting that newly imported Africans lived for at least that long after their disembarkation. This certainly coincides with Vincent Brown's comparison of Europeans living in West Africa. See Burnard, *Mastery, Tyranny, and Desire*, 17; Brown, *The Reaper's Garden*, 2. For more recent work on slave mortality rates in Jamaica, see Forster and Smith, "Surviving Slavery."

19. Michael Craton in "Jamaican Slave Mortality" asserts that enslaved Creoles lived into their thirties in the mid-1700s and into their forties by 1830, while George Roberts asserts that the average life expectancy for an enslaved Creole was only 22.8 years in the 1830s, and by the 1840s, during the postemancipation era, this life expectancy rate rose to forty ("A Life Table for a West Indian Enslaved Population"). See also Riley, *Poverty and Life Expectancy*, 23.

20. Curtin, *The Atlantic Slave Trade*, 59. Curtin goes on to argue that Jamaica's

enslaved population experienced a natural decrease of 6.7 percent per year (58). Burnard found similar numbers: 120,000 slaves lived in Jamaica in 1750, and that number rose to only 300,000 by 1800 (*Mastery, Tyranny, and Desire*, 15). I will discuss the nature of slave increase and decrease further in chapters 2 and 4.

21. DU, Stephen Fuller to Lord Hawksbury, May 4, 1788, Stephen Fuller Papers.

22. The West Indian Lobby, also called the West Indian Interest, comprised island agents (men appointed by their colonial governments to represent British West Indian interests in Parliament), London merchants engaged in the West Indian trade, absentee planters living in England, and ministers of Parliament with West Indian connections and interests. O'Shaughnessy, "The Formation of a Commercial Lobby," 72. For more on the West Indian Lobby, see Penson, "The London West India Interest"; Higman, "The West India Interest in Parliament."

23. UWI, Journals of the Assembly of Jamaica, vol. 8, fol. 428. Assemblymen also attributed the natural decrease of the enslaved population to female promiscuity, abortions, and high infant and child mortality.

24. Ibid; Fuller, *Report, Resolutions, and Remonstrance*, 9.

25. See Vasconcellos, "From Chattel to Breeding Wenches."

26. Another bill passed the House of Commons in 1805 but failed to pass the House of Lords. Parliament did vote to abolish the slave trade on March 25, 1807.

27. See Vasconcellos, "From Chattel to Breeding Wenches."

28. The Dolben's Act of 1788, proposed by noted abolitionist Sir William Dolben, was not designed to end the trade but to restrict it and, theoretically, to improve conditions aboard ship. The act mandated that no more than two-fifths of a ship's cargo be children and limited the number of African men to one male per ship ton. Meant to restrict the trade, the act actually had an adverse effect. Since it did not define *child*, more children between the ages of twelve and eighteen entered the trade, and planters fervently began debating the benefits of breeding slaves rather than buying them. With the limitation on the number of African men aboard ship, this act also led to an increased number of girls in the trade. See Vasconcellos, "From Chattel to Breeding Wenches." For more on the Dolben's Act, see LoGerfo, "Sir William Dolben and 'The Cause of Humanity.'"

29. Mathison, *Notices Respecting Jamaica*, 12.

30. See Williams, *Capitalism and Slavery*; Anstey, "Capitalism and Slavery: A Critique"; Engerman, "The Slave Trade and British Capital Formation"; Drescher, *Econocide*; Carrington and Drescher, "Debate"; Drescher, "The Decline Thesis"; Eltis, *Economic Growth and the Ending of the Transatlantic Slave Trade*; Drescher, *Capitalism and Anti-Slavery*; Holt, "Explaining Abolition"; Bender, *The Anti-Slavery Debate*; Pemberton and Samaroo, "Eric Williams," vols. 1 and 2; Cateau and Carrington, *Capitalism and Slavery Fifty Year's Later*; Carrington, "Capitalism and Slavery and Caribbean Historiography"; Reid and Ryden, "Sugar, Land Markets, and the Williams Thesis."

31. See King, *Stolen Childhood*.

32. Ibid., xx.

33. Schwartz, *Born in Bondage*, 4.

34. Kiple, *The Caribbean Slave*; Sheridan, *Doctors and Slaves*; Steckel, "A Peculiar Population"; Kiple, "The Nutritional Link"; Bush, "Hard Labor." For more recent work on slave infant and child mortality and slave fertility, see Coelho and McGuire, "Diets

versus Diseases"; Steckel, "Diets versus Diseases"; Tadman, "The Demographic Cost of Sugar"; Follett, "Heat, Sex, and Sugar"; Morgan, "Slave Women and Reproduction"; Turner, "Home-grown Slaves."

35. See Mair, *Women Field Workers*; Morrissey, *Slave Women in the New World*; Bush, *Slave Women in Caribbean Society*; Beckles, *Natural Rebels*; Beckles, *Centering Woman*. For more recent works on slave women in the Caribbean, see Moitt, *Women and Slavery in the French Antilles*; Morgan, *Laboring Women*; Altink, *Representations of Slave Women*.

36. See Goveia, *Slave Society in the British Leeward Islands*; Higman, "Household Structure and Fertility on Jamaican Slave Plantations"; Higman, "The Slave Family and Household in the British West Indies"; Higman, "African and Creole Slave Family Patterns in Trinidad.". See also Craton, "Changing Patterns of Slave Families in the British West Indies"; Lamur, "The Slave Family"; Welch, "The Slave Family in the Urban Context"; Stark, "Discovering the Invisible Puerto Rican Slave Family"; Green, "'A Civil Inconvenience'?"; Hawthorne, "'Being now, as it were, one family.'"

37. See Blake, "A History of Children in Nineteenth Century Jamaica."

38. See King, *Stolen Childhood*.

1 / "To so dark a destiny"

The title of this chapter is from "The Slave Mother's Address," 4.

1. Trelawny, *An Essay Concerning Slavery*, 34–35.

2. Ibid., 4–6.

3. Beckford, *Remarks Upon the Situation of Negroes in Jamaica*, 24–25.

4. Burnard, *Mastery, Tyranny, and Desire*, 17.

5. Ramsay, *An Essay on the Treatment and Conversion of African Slaves*, 97. The emphasis is Ramsay's.

6. For more on the slave trade to Jamaica, see Klein, "The English Slave Trade to Jamaica"; McDonald, "Measuring the British Slave Trade to Jamaica"; Burnard and Morgan, "The Dynamics of the Slave Market"; Mouser, *A Slaving Voyage to Africa and Jamaica*; Vasconcellos, "From Chattel to Breeding Wenches"; Diptee, *From Africa to Jamaica*.

7. NLJ, Spring Vale Journal and Accounts.

8. Craton and Walvin, *A Jamaican Plantation*, 130; JA, Worthy Park Estate.

9. Although enslaved women preferred these tasks to working in the fields, their lives as domestics were not as privileged as one may think. Dr. George Pinkard, a visitor to the region in the 1790s, argued that their duties required the same amount of physical exertion as those of field women. He also noted their severe punishments. See Pinkard, *Notes on the West Indies*, 258.

10. Moreton, *Manners and Customs*, 152.

11. UWI, Thomas Thistlewood Diaries, September 22, 1759, Monson 31/10. For more on Thistlewood, see Hall, "The Diary of a Westmoreland Planter: Part 1"; Hall, "The Diary of a Westmoreland Planter: Conclusion"; Hall, *In Miserable Slavery*; Burnard, *Mastery, Tyranny, and Desire*.

12. In 1816 the Jamaican Assembly limited the number of lashes to thirty-nine, no matter the age of the slave. In 1826 the Assembly prohibited the flogging of women. See JA, Laws of Jamaica, 57 George III, c. 25 (1816), 7 George IV, c. 23 (1826).

13. Craton, *Searching for the Invisible Man*, 87; Morgan, "Slave Women and

Reproduction," 249. According to Ian Gregory, infant and child mortality rates among white children living in Britain were high during this period as well, fluctuating between one and two deaths out of every ten live births. Income, class, and location all played factors. According to David Cutler, Angus Denton, and Adriana Lleras-Muney, those rates began to improve somewhat beginning in the 1750s for European children. For American children the rates began to decline around 1790. They attribute the change to a decline in infectious diseases; increased vaccination, public health, urbanization, and industrialization; and improved nutrition. Gregory has noted that this decline picked up speed the 1850s. See Gregory, "Different Places, Different Stories," 774; Cutler et al., "The Determinates of Mortality."

14. Higman, *Slave Population and Economy in Jamaica*, 49.

15. Morgan, "Slave Women and Reproduction," 248.

16. Klein and Engerman, "Fertility Differentials," 370–71. For more on breastfeeding practices, see Handler and Corruccini, "Weaning among West Indian Slaves"; Morgan, "Slave Women and Reproduction"; Follett, "Heat, Sex, and Sugar."

17. Kiple, *The Caribbean Slave*, 123–24.

18. Sheridan, "Mortality and the Medical Treatment of Slaves," 199.

19. NLJ, John Poole to Richard Elletson, January 2, 1775, Roger Hope Elletson Letterbook.

20. NLJ, Anna Eliza Elletson to John Poole and Edward East, January 23, 1777, Roger Hope Elletson Letterbook. Richard Elletson died in 1775 and left his estate to Anna Eliza in its entirety. Rather than sell the estate, she chose to administer it as an absentee planter and landlord. In 1778 she married Henry Brydges, Duke of Chandos, making her the Duchess of Chandos. For more on Anna Eliza and her administration of Hope Estate, see Sturtz, "The 'Dim Duke' and Duchess Chandos."

21. NLJ, Anna Eliza Elletson to John Poole and Edward East, August 5, 1778, Roger Hope Elletson Letterbook. Despite Poole and the Duchess of Chandos's wishes, Hope Estate managers seemed to habitually stop providing the children with meals when provisions became low. Poole continued to push the issue. See NLJ, John Poole to the Duchess of Chandos, September 10, 1778, Roger Hope Elletson Letterbook.

22. UWI, Ezekiel Dickenson to Edward East and Caleb Dickenson, January 31, 1778, Letterbook of Ezekiel Dickenson, 1777–88, Dickenson Family Papers, MR 515.

23. UWI, "1784 Instructions," Slebach Collection, MR 541.

24. CL, J. Fowler to James Stothert, April 12, 1787, July 15, 1787, September 7, 1787, James Stothert Papers.

25. DU, Stephen Fuller to the Honourable Committee of Correspondence, May 16, 1788, Stephen Fuller Papers.

26. Great Britain, Parliament, House of Commons, *House of Commons Sessional Papers*, 61; UWI, Journals of the Assembly of Jamaica, vol. 8, fols. 430, 434–35, MR 3720; Fuller, *Notes on the Two Reports*, 26–33.

27. UWI, Journals of the Assembly of Jamaica, vol. 8, fols. 435, 434, MR 3720.

28. For more on medicine on Jamaica's plantations and estates, see Craton, "Death, Disease and Medicine"; Sheridan, *Doctors and Slaves*; Sheridan, "Slave Medicine in Jamaica"; Payne-Jackson and Alleyne, *Jamaican Folk Medicine*; Thornton, "Coerced Care." For the wider Caribbean, see Handler, "Slave Medicine and Obeah"; Handler, "Diseases and Medical Disabilities"; De Barros, "'Setting Things Right'"; Harrison, *Medicine in an Age of Commerce and Empire*; Jensen, *For the Health of the Enslaved.*

29. UWI, Journals of the Assembly of Jamaica, vol. 8, fol. 435, MR 3720.

30. UWI, Thomas Thistlewood Diaries, June 6, 1752, Monson 31/3.

31. See Vasconcellos, "From Chattel to Breeding Wenches."

32. UWI, Thomas Thistlewood Diaries, March 1, 1754, Monson 31/3.

33. UWI, "Negro and Stock Accounts on York Plantation, 1778–1837," Gale-Morant Family Papers.

34. Collins, *Practical Rules*, 135. For more on slave infanticide, see Morgan, "Slave Women and Reproduction"; Altink, "'I Did Not Want to Face the Shame of Exposure'"; Clover, "'This horably wicked action.'"

35. *A Speech Delivered at a Free Conference*, 31; British Parliamentary Papers, "Evidence of Robert Hibbert," 368. According to Hibbert, an eighteen-year resident of Jamaica, there was not a single year on his estates when the number of births outweighed the number of deaths. However, he did note that the enslaved population increased by natural means at a rate of 2.5 percent (364, 368).

36. *The Speech of Sir William Young*, 43.

37. See Vasconcellos, "From Chattel to Breeding Wenches."

38. For more on British amelioration policies, see Ward, *British West Indian Slavery*; Luster, *The Amelioration of the Slaves*; Dunkley, *Agency of the Enslaved*; Fergus, "The *Siete Partidas*."

39. JA, Laws of Jamaica, 29 George III, c. 2 (1788). The Jamaican Assembly revised these laws every few years, although the majority remained unchanged. See 41 George III, c. 26 (1801), 50 George III, c. 16 (1810), 57 George III, c. 25 (1816), 7 George IV, c. 23 (1826), 6 George IV, c. 19 (1831).

40. UWI, Journals of the Assembly of Jamaica, vol. 8, fol. 428, 431, MR 3720. If auditors discovered instances of natural decrease or increase that were not reported, they fined physicians 20 pounds colonial currency rather than pounds sterling for each instance; 1.4 pounds colonial currency equaled £1 sterling throughout the entire period of my study. See UWI, Journals of the Assembly of Jamaica, vol. 8, fol. 428, 431, MR 3720; Higman, *Slave Population and Economy in Jamaica*, xx.

41. Jamaica, House of Assembly, *The New Consolidated Act*, 9.

42. Lewis, *Journal of a West India Proprietor*, 79.

43. UWI, Bernard and William Dickenson to Thomas S. Salmon, December 1, 1792, Dickenson Family Letterbook, 1792–94, Dickenson Family Papers, MR 518.

44. UWI, Rowland Fearon to Lord Penrhyn, January 26, 1805, Penrhyn Castle Papers.

45. Jamaica, House of Assembly, *An Act for the Better Order and Government of Slaves*, 29; JA, Laws of Jamaica, 41 George III, c. 26 (1801). The law remained in effect until August 1834.

46. Lewis, *Journal of a West Indian Proprietor*, 79.

47. Ibid., 42, 133.

48. JA, Braco Estate.

49. NLJ, *Columbian Magazine* 2 (1797): 263, 328, C652.

50. De la Beche, *Notes on the Present Condition of the Negroes*, 12. *Lying-in* is the term given by Jamaican planters to this four- to six-month maternity leave granted to slave mothers who recently gave birth.

51. Beckford, *Remarks Upon the Situation of Negroes in Jamaica*, 37.

52. NLJ, Charles Gordon Gray to Father, June 8, 1815, Gray Correspondence.

53. See UWI, Gale-Morant Family Papers; UWI, Slebach Collection, MR 543; NLJ, Somerset Plantation; NLJ, Spring Vale Journal and Accounts; Marsden, *An Account of the Island of Jamaica*, 39; Long, *The History of Jamaica*, 2: 436.

54. Lewis, *Journal of a West Indian Proprietor*, 146.

55. See also Laborie, *The Coffee Planter of Saint Domingo*; Marsden, *An Account of the Island of Jamaica*; M'Neill, *Observations on the Treatment of the Negroes*; Dancer, *The Medical Assistant*; Roughly, *The Jamaica Planter's Guide*.

56. For children in Jamaica, see Maclean, *Children of Jamaica*; Blake, "The Child on the Radnor Plantation"; Blake, "A History of Children in Nineteenth Century Jamaica"; Diptee, *From Africa to Jamaica*; Vasconcellos, "From Chattel to Breeding Wenches."

57. Gardner, *A History of Jamaica*, 97, 180, 382. For yabbawares, see Mathewson, "Archaeological Analysis of Material Culture"; Armstrong, *The Old Village and the Great House*; Meyers, "West African Tradition in the Decoration of Colonial Jamaican Folk Pottery."

58. See Goveia, *Slave Society in the British Leeward Islands*; Higman, "Household Structure and Fertility on Jamaican Slave Plantations"; Higman, "The Slave Family and Household." For more on slave family and kinship in Jamaica, see Patterson, "From Endo-deme to Matri-deme"; Craton, "Changing Patterns of Slave Families in the British West Indies"; Olwig, "Finding a Place for the Slave Family"; Besson, "The Creolization of African-American Slave Kinship"; Besson, "Euro-Creole, Afro-Creole, Meso-Creole"; and Saunders, "Free and Enslaved African Communities."

59. See Burnard, *Mastery, Tyranny, and Desire*, 189.

60. Lewis, *Journal of a West Indian Proprietor*, 219. For more on the relationship between shipmates, see Mullin, *Africa in America*; Warner-Lewis, *Central Africa in the Caribbean*; and Hawthorne, "'Being now, as it were, one family.'"

61. Renny, *An History of Jamaica*, 172. The emphasis is Renny's.

62. Kelly, *Jamaica in 1831*, 40.

63. Sells, *Remarks on the Condition of the Slaves*, 28.

64. Ibid.

65. Lewis, *Journal of a West Indian Proprietor*, 109.

66. JA, Registry of the Returns of Slaves, Westmoreland, 1B/11/7/1.

67. Lewis, *Journal of a West Indian Proprietor*, 109.

68. NLJ, "Hope Estate, in the Parish of St. Andrew, Jamaica," *Jamaica Journal* 1 (1818): 19.

69. Higman, "The Slave Family and Household," 278. Recent archeological excavations and findings support Higman's arguments. See Delle and Hauser, *Out of Many, One People*.

70. UWI, Thomas Thistlewood Diaries, September 8, 1761, Monson 31/12. For Nanny's repeated acts of running away without her child, see the remaining entries for this volume of Thistlewood's diary. Nanny never succeeded in successfully absconding from Egypt, as she is still listed in the inventories in 1770. By 1786, twenty-five years later, she is one of three slaves listed as living alone on the estate. It is not known whether Thistlewood eventually purchased her from Cunningham or whether Cunningham continued to hire her out to Egypt. See UWI, Thomas Thistlewood Diaries, Monson 31/12–31/35; Burnard, *Mastery, Tyranny, and Desire*, 185, 188.

71. JA, Registry of the Returns of Slaves, St. Thomas in the Vale, 1B/11/7/15. It is

not known if Roxanna's escape was successful or what became of her or the children after their escape.

72. NLJ, Radnor Plantation.

73. NLJ, *Royal Gazette*, September 18, 1824.

74. JA, Laws of Jamaica, 8 George II, c. 5 (1735).

75. NLJ, Duke of Manchester Accounts.

76. Great Britain, Parliament, Agency Anti-Slavery Committee, *The Condition of the Slave*, 2.

77. NLJ, *Royal Gazette*, February 23, 1782–March 2, 1782.

78. JA, Journal of Benjamin Scott Moncrieffe, 1A/5/2/26.

79. NLJ, Francis Graham to Rowland Alston, September 6, 1816, Georgia Estate Letterbook.

80. JA, Laws of Jamaica, 8 George II, c. 5 (1818). This law also protected children from outside relationships, or those who were adopted.

81. UWI, Journals of the Assembly of Jamaica, vol. 13, fol. 580, MR 3721.

82. Collins, *Practical Rules*, 143; Roughly, *The Jamaica Planter's Guide*, 103; Stewart, *A View of the Past and Present State*, 312; Mathison, *Notices Respecting Jamaica*, 91.

83. The 1826 Consolidated Slave Law outlawed the branding of slaves. See JA, Laws of Jamaica, 7 George IV, c. 23 (1826).

84. Renny, *An History of Jamaica*, 176. See also NLJ, Charles Gordon Gray to Father, January 5, 1809, March 11, 1814, Gray Correspondence; Roughly, *The Jamaica Planter's Guide*, 105.

85. Roughly, *The Jamaica Planter's Guide*, 107. Plantation and estate journals frequently list children receiving hoes and baskets along with the other slaves. See JA, Braco Estate; JA, "List of Slaves on Green Castle Pen with Their Age, Occupation, & Condition on the 1st January 1834," Kelly Family Papers, 4/43/8; JA, Green Park Estate, 4/8/2–3; JA, Harmony Hall Estate, 7/56/1–4, 7; NLJ, Carlton Estate; NLJ, Moorshall Estate.

86. JA, Braco Estate.

87. JA, Green Park Estate, 4/8/2–3. See also JA, Rose Hall Estate, 1B/26/1–3.

88. Roughly, *The Jamaica Planter's Guide*, 107.

89. JA, "List of Slaves on Green Castle Pen with Their Age, Occupation, & Condition on the 1st January 1834," Kelly Family Papers, 4/43/8; JA, Green Park Estate, 4/8/2–3; JA, Rose Hall Estate, 1B/26/1–3; NLJ, Radnor Plantation.

90. CL, J. Fowler to John Stothert, January 8, 1789, James Stothert Papers.

91. It is important to note differences in terminology in North American and Jamaican white society. While North American whites assigned the term *people of color* or *colored* to those in both the black and the mulatto communities in North America, whether slave or free, Jamaican whites used these terms along with *mulatto* strictly for those who contained some degree of white blood. Jamaican blacks were categorized as negro or black. When speaking of the free or enslaved colored communities as a whole, white society categorized everyone as mulatto. Only when a specific person was mentioned were specific identifiers such as *quadroon*, *mustee*, or *negro* assigned.

92. Dunn, "The Story of Two Jamaican Slaves," 190–91. For more on these odds, see Dunn, "'Dreadful Idlers' in the Cane Fields"; Dunn, "Sugar Production and Slave Women in Jamaica."

93. Shepherd, "Ethnicity, Colour, and Gender," 205. Shepherd explains that there was a distinct gender bias in the allocation of domestic work. Women and girls worked in child care, sewing, cooking, and laundry, while men and boys served as grooms, butlers, valets, and gardeners.

94. UWI, Thomas Thistlewood Diaries, October 1, 1752, May 2, 1762, Monson 31/3. Douglas Hall and Trevor Burnard both note that Doll sent Sally back to Thistlewood in October 1765 because she was not minding her work and so was unable to develop the seamstress skills Thistlewood desired from her. Thistlewood put the girl in the stocks, then sent her to the fields. Sally became quite the troublemaker, an undoubted response to her situation and frequent sexual attacks by Thistlewood, and ran away with some degree of regularity; the first instance occurred not long after being placed in the stocks at the young age of nine or ten. Even at this young age she refused to accept her situation. Burnard gives an excellent but sad account of Sally's troubled life on Egypt, painting the picture of a slave whose anger at her situation became so consuming that she was even shunned by the slave community itself. Unable to deal with her frequent running away, acts of theft, and self-destruction, Thistlewood had Sally transported off the island in November 1784. It is unknown what became of her after that. See Hall, *In Miserable Slavery*, 137; Burnard, *Mastery, Tyranny and Desire*, 218–21.

95. Stewart, *An Account of Jamaica and Its Inhabitants*, 161.

96. JA, Votes of the Assembly, 1791–92, fol. 109.

97. Riland, *Memoirs of a West Indian Planter*, 3.

98. Stewart, *View of the Past and Present State*, 171. The emphasis is Stewart's.

99. UWI, Thomas Thistlewood Diaries, March 9, 1767, Monson 31/18.

100. Stewart, *View of the Past and Present State*, 267.

101. NLJ, St. Ann Slave Court.

102. See UWI, Thomas Thistlewood Diaries, Monson 31/1–31/35.

103. See JA, Port Royal Summary Slave Trials, 2/19/30; NLJ, St. Ann Slave Court.

104. Lewis, *Journal of a West Indian Proprietor*, 110–11. According to Lewis, Minetta gave her owner the poison in some brandy with water. In her defense, she argued that she had taken it from the medicine chest and did not know it to be poison and that her grandmother told her to give it to him. Lewis believed her to be lying, as she "stood by the bed to see her master drink the poison; witnessed his agonies without one expression of surprise or pity" (111).

105. Phillippo, *Jamaica*, 96.

106. UWI, Thomas Thistlewood Diaries, July 7, 1754, Monson 31/5.

107. Sally's exact age is unknown; however, she is estimated to be either nine or ten at the time of her purchase. She began running away almost immediately (ibid., Monson 31/3–35; Burnard, *Mastery, Tyranny and Desire*, 218–21).

108. NLJ, *Royal Gazette*, December 10, 1779. For more on enslaved children and resistance in Jamaica, see Jones, "'If This Be Living."

109. JA, Robert Sewell to the Honourable Committee of Correspondence, December 27, 1796, June 6, 1797, Committee of Correspondence, Letterbook, 1B/4/14/2.

110. *Reasons for Establishing a Registry of Slaves*, 40, 56, 64; *A Review of the Reasons Given for Establishing a Registry of Slaves*, 9, 20–21; JA, Laws of Jamaica, 57 George III, c. 15 (1816).

111. See JA, Laws of Jamaica, 57 George III, c. 15 (1816). This fine would have been paid in Jamaican colonial currency rather than British pounds sterling.

112. Lewis, *Journal of a West Indian Proprietor*, 54, 237. For similar complaints see Marsden, *An Account of the Island of Jamaica*, 40; NLJ, Anna Eliza Elletson to John Poole and Edward East, August 5, 1778, Roger Hope Elletson Letterbook; NLJ, William Adlam to John Wemyss, February 1, 1820, Letterbook of John Wemyss; UWI, Dickenson Family Papers, MR 515, 518, 2599–600, 2950–53; UWI, Slebach Collection, MR 527–29.

113. JA, Rose Hall Estate, 1B/26/3.

114. NLJ, Maryland Estate.

115. NLJ, Radnor Plantation.

116. Roberts, *Population of Jamaica*, 3.

117. Higman, *Slave Population and Economy in Jamaica*, 47.

118. Ibid., 257.

2 / "The child whom many fathers share"

The title of this chapter is from NLJ, *Columbian Magazine* 1 (1796): 119, C652.

1. JA, Votes of the Assembly, 1794–95, fols. 79–80, 119.

2. Long, *The History of Jamaica*, 2: 333.

3. Edwards, *History of Jamaica*, 2. According to Catherine Hall, the white population fell to fifteen thousand by 1834, while the number of free blacks and free people of color rose to forty-five thousand (*Civilising Subjects*, 74). Higman places the white population at 16,750 in 1832, with 8,500 whites living in the urban areas (*Slave Population and Economy in Jamaica*, 144).

4. Madden, *Twelvemonths Residence*, 114.

5. Edwards, *History of Jamaica*, 17.

6. Higman, *Slave Population and Economy*, 142; Hall, *Civilising Subjects*, 77–78. The exact number of free blacks and free people of color is difficult to ascertain. Edward Long estimates that thirty-seven thousand lived in Jamaica in the late eighteenth century (*The History of Jamaica*, 1: 377). However, the island did not begin a systematic census of the enslaved population until the Registries began in 1817.

7. Patterson, *Sociology of Slavery*, 146. Higman agrees with these figures, arguing that 37 percent of enslaved Jamaicans were African-born in 1817 (*Slave Population and Economy*, 75–76).

8. Hall, *Civilising Subjects*, 78.

9. Van der Berghe, *Race and Racism*, 22. For more on race and social stratification in the Caribbean, see Alleyne, *The Construction and Representation of Race and Ethnicity*; Clarke, *Decolonizing the Colonial City*; Murdoch, "A Legacy of Trauma."

10. Madden, *Twelvemonths Residence*, 113.

11. Hall, *Civilising Subjects*, 78.

12. Until 1796 they could not give evidence against any person of color in court. The Jamaican Assembly extended that privilege to court cases involving members of the white community in 1813. See JA, Laws of Jamaica, 36 George III, c. 23 (1796), 54 George III, c. 19 (1813).

13. Brathwaite, *The Development of Creole Society in Jamaica*, 171. For more on free blacks, free people of color, and the law, see Jordan, "American Chiaroscuro"; Hurwitz and Hurwitz, "A Token of Freedom"; Small, "Racial Group Boundaries and Identities"; Sio, "Marginality and Free Coloured Identity"; Petley, "'Legitimacy' and Social Boundaries"; Paton, *No Bond but the Law*.

14. UWI, Journals of the Assembly of Jamaica, vol. 5, fol. 291, , vol. 8, fol. 429, MR 3719; Long, *The History of Jamaica*, 2: 321.

15. Hall, *Civilising Subjects*, 73, 72.

16. Williamson, *Medical and Miscellaneous Observations*, 49. For more on this practice, see Hall, *In Miserable Slavery*; Burnard, "The Sexual Life of an Eighteenth Century Jamaican Slave Overseer"; Stoler, *Carnal Knowledge and Imperial Power*; Wickstrom, "The Politics of Forbidden Liaisons"; Altink, "Forbidden Fruit"; Burnard, *Mastery, Tyranny, and Desire*; Newman, "Gender, Sexuality and the Formation of Racial Identities."

17. Phillippo, *Jamaica*, 53.

18. See UWI, Thomas Thistlewood Diaries, 1750–86, Monson 31/1–31; and Hall, *In Miserable Slavery*. A bit, or Spanish *real*, equaled about 7½ pence in Jamaica colonial currency. Therefore Thistlewood would have given them 1 shilling 3 pence currency and 2 shillings 6 pence currency, respectively. See Flügel and Grund, *The Merchant's Assistant*, 307.

19. Hall, *In Miserable Slavery*, 28.

20. See Burnard, *Mastery, Tyranny, and Desire*, 156–62.

21. Moreton, *Manners and Customs*, 77, 90. See also the testimony of Reverend J. Barry before the House of Lords Committee on the condition and treatment of slaves in 1832 in Legion, *A Second Letter*, 39.

22. NLJ, *Postscript to the Royal Gazette*, June 18–25, 1791.

23. Burnard, *Mastery, Tyranny, and Desire*, 232.

24. JA, Laws of Jamaica, 57 George III, c. 25 (1816). By 1831 that punishment could be applied to any abuse on a female slave under ten (6 George IV, c. 19 [1831]).

25. M'Mahon, *Jamaica Plantership*, 51.

26. Gardner, *A History of Jamaica*, 264.

27. Nugent, *Lady Nugent's Journal*, 87. For more on Lady Nugent, see Winter, "Lady Nugent's Journal"; Brandenstein, "'Making "the agreeable" to the big wigs.'"

28. UWI, Thomas Thistlewood Diaries, July 7, 1751, July 6, 1751, Monson 31/2; Hall, *In Miserable Slavery*, 18. Thistlewood's relationship with Marina ended when he left Vineyard Pen. He never mentioned her again, adding more proof to the common belief that these women were merely sexual objects to be used at their owner's whim for as long as he desired. Once he finished with her, he moved on to the next woman without a second thought. Only on rare occasions did these relationships mean more to the planter, estate manager, or bookkeeper. For more on gifts and the wider consideration of the slave mistress, see the contemporary novel *Busha's Mistress* by Cyrus Francis Perkins.

29. UWI, Thomas Thistlewood Diaries, February 24, 1751, Monson 31/7; Hall, *In Miserable Slavery*, 71. Burnard is quick to point out that Myrtilla's relationship with Crookshanks did not give her automatic protection. Thistlewood was often dismissive of Crookshanks's behavior toward Myrtilla, accusing him of coddling his favorite. When Myrtilla miscarried in February 1755, Thistlewood was quick to counter Crookshanks's claims that the child was his by assigning fatherhood to Salt River Quaw, one of Thistlewood's field slaves. While her status as mistress or concubine might elevate her status in the eyes of her benefactor, it did not change a slave's status with the white community as a whole. See Burnard, *Mastery, Tyranny, and Desire*, 98.

30. Lewis, *Journal of a West India Proprietor*, 52.

31. For the most thorough discussion of the relationships between white men and slave women in the Caribbean, see the many works of Hilary Beckles. For a North American perspective, see Jennings, "'Us Colored Women Had to Go through A Plenty'"; Yarbrough, "Power, Perception, and Interracial Sex."

32. UWI, Thomas Thistlewood Diaries, July 24, 1765, Monson 31/16; Hall, *In Miserable Slavery*, 137. Phibbah was not owned by Thistlewood himself. Mary Cope, the wife of his employer, neighbor, and fellow planter John Cope, owned Phibbah. According to Thistlewood, Phibbah had given birth three times: to Coobah, a daughter by an unknown enslaved man; to a stillbirth in 1755, who Thistlewood said was Phibbah's child by Cope; and to Thistlewood's son John, who was born in April 1760 and manumitted on May 3, 1762. Phibbah's own manumission did not come until November 26, 1792, a few years after Thistlewood's death in 1786. See JA, Manumissions Liber, 1760–65, 1772, fol. 119, 1B/11/6/7; Hall, *In Miserable Slavery*, 314; Burnard, *Mastery, Tyranny, and Desire*, 229. For more on Phibbah, as well as Thistlewood's relationship with her, see Burnard, *Mastery, Tyranny, and Desire*, 228–40.

33. UWI, Thomas Thistlewood Diaries, July 24, 1765, Monson 31/16; Hall, *In Miserable Slavery*, 137; Burnard, *Mastery, Tyranny, and Desire*, 57, 232. Mrs. Bennett stipulated that Bess's ownership, as well as that of her future children, was to pass on to John at his mother's death. According to Burnard, Bess had two children (*Mastery, Tyranny, and Desire*, 57).

34. See UWI, Thomas Thistlewood Diaries, 1772, Monson 31/23. See also Hall, *In Miserable Slavery*.

35. Burnard, *Mastery, Tyranny, and Desire*, 235.

36. Nugent, *Lady Nugent's Journal*, 29.

37. Ibid., 12.

38. CL, Memoir of Charles Machin, fol. 61.

39. Hinton, ed., *Memoir of William Knibb*, 50. Missionaries weren't the only ones to complain about the white population. Absentee owners were well known to lament their unfavorable experiences with their overseers and bookkeepers, who all had horrible reputations for mismanagement, negligence, and misconduct. According to Richard Pares, absentees were lucky to find an overseer they could trust; most asked a neighbor, friend, or attorney to look in on estate management as supervisors (*A West India Fortune*, 18–20). See also Hall, "Absentee-Proprietorship in the British West Indies," 15.

40. JA, George Turner to M. D. Hodgson, September 13, 1791, October 26, 1791, Tweedie Family Papers, 4/45/66.

41. JA, Michael Hanley to Lord Balthurst, September 22, 1823, Dispatches, England to Jamaica, 1B/5/18.

42. JA, Registry of the Returns of Slaves, St. David, 1B/11/7/25.

43. *Marly*, 94.

44. Corry, *Observations Upon the Windward Coast of Africa*, 152.

45. Ibid., 50; Gardner, *A History of Jamaica*, 381; Marsden, *An Account of the Island of Jamaica*, 38; Cooper, *Facts Illustrative of the Condition of the Negro Slaves in Jamaica*, 26. For more on this practice, see Beckles, "Creolisation in Action"; Dunn, "The Demographic Contrast between Slave Life in Jamaica and Virginia"; Newman, "Gender, Sexuality and the Formation of Racial Identities"; Newman, "Contesting 'Black' Liberty and Subjecthood."

46. Shepherd, "Ethnicity, Colour, and Gender," 205.

47. Lewis, *Journal of a West Indian Proprietor*, 105.

48. Ibid., 68–69. For more on manumission, see Engerman, "Pricing Freedom"; Kleijwegt, *The Faces of Freedom*; Brana-Shute and Sparks, *Paths to Freedom*.

49. See, NLJ, Francis Graham to Thomas Mills, December 10, 1807, Georgia Estate Letterbook; NLJ, Edward East to the Duchess of Chandos, May 24, 1779, Roger Hope Elletson Letterbook; JA, Votes of the Assembly, 1808–9, fols. 20, 102. Edward Kamau Brathwaite argues that Jamaican law stipulated that octoroons, the children of a quinteroon and a white man, were declared free at birth. Lewis, however, stated that quinteroons were free by law. I have not yet found a copy of this law. See Brathwaite, *The Development of Creole Society in Jamaica*, 167; Lewis, *Journal of a West Indian Proprietor*, 68.

50. See, JA, Manumissions Liber, 1772–74, 1B/11/6/8.

51. Nugent, *Lady Nugent's Journal*, 69.

52. Lewis, *Journal of a West India Proprietor*, 68.

53. Moreton, *Manners and Customs*, 106. Edward Long noted the shock of newcomers to the island when they saw the same (*The History of Jamaica*, 2: 86).

54. Higman, "Household Structure and Fertility on Jamaican Slave Plantations," 536.

55. NLJ, Harmony Hall Estate, MS 1652. It is interesting that Kate is classified as being black rather than sambo, as many other children of black and mulatto parents would be labeled. This suggests that Harmony Hall management was less open to utilizing the numerous degrees of whiteness listed in Table 2 as other estate owners and managers. It also proves that these racial classifications were subjective, not uniform across the island.

56. Williams, *A Tour Through the Island of Jamaica*, 27.

57. Fanon, *Black Skin, White Masks*, 59. See also Murdoch, "A Legacy of Trauma"; Newman, "Contesting 'Black' Liberty and Subjecthood."

58. Lewis, *Journal of a West Indian Proprietor*, 52, 53.

59. Moreton, *Manners and Customs*, 125.

60. JA, Thetford Plantation Books, 4/23/9–11.

61. As I will discuss further in chapter 4, all children under six, regardless of their color, received their freedom with abolition. Children seven and older were classified as apprentices like their parents.

62. It is interesting that one of Susanna's children was christened William Pengilly. Although Susanna is ten years older than Elizabeth Pengilly, it is possible that they are connected in some way. Worthy Park and Thetford were owned by the same person and shifted staff back and forth between the two estates. Furthermore, the two estates neighbor each other in the parish of St. John. Perhaps Pengilly was a bookkeeper on Worthy Park before moving to Thetford. It is also possible that Pengilly went back to Worthy Park after leaving Thetford, as twenty-four-year-old Rippon chose the Christian name William Pengilly in 1822. Or perhaps Pengilly is just a popular name at Worthy Park. See JA, Worthy Park Estate, 4/23/1–7.

63. Moreton, *Manners and Customs*, 79, 93; Stewart, *View of the Past and Present State*, 194; Beckford, *A Descriptive Account of the Island of Jamaica*, 379.

64. Moreton, *Manners and Customs*, 97.

65. See JA, Laws of Jamaica, 15 George III, c. 18 (1774); JA, Manumissions Liber, 1774, fol. 1, 1B/11/6/11; Davis, *The West Indies*, 72.

66. For more on the difficulties surrounding manumission, see Campbell, "How Free Is Free?"

67. It is quite possible that Thistlewood had a child by Nago Hannah, who gave birth to a mulatto girl on June 30, 1754. He was with her frequently in September and October 1753. In August 1754 Nago Jenny, a favorite of Thistlewood's, gave birth to a mulatto boy. In September 1755, she gave birth to another mulatto boy she named Quaw but later called Little Thomas. Mountain Lucy told Thistlewood she was pregnant with his child in October 1755, but he could not be certain whether the child was indeed his. Phibbah, as I have already discussed, gave birth to Thistlewood's son John in 1760, but gave birth to a stillborn child in 1755 that Thistlewood did not claim. See UWI, Thomas Thistlewood Diaries, 1753–55, Monson 31/4–31/6.

68. UWI, Thomas Thistlewood Diaries, 1765, Monson 31/16; Burnard, *Mastery, Tyranny, and Desire,* 53–54.

69. Burnard, *Mastery, Tyranny, and Desire,* 235.

70. NLJ, Edward East to the Duchess of Chandos, May 24, 1774, Roger Hope Elletson Letterbook.

71. NLJ, John Concannon to the Duchess of Chandos, March 20, 1779, Roger Hope Elletson Letterbook.

72. UWI, James Concannon to Maria Eliza Elletson, May 3, 1779, January 20, 1780, Stowe Collection.

73. NLJ, Anna Eliza Elletson to John Poole and Edward East, March 12, 1780, Roger Hope Elletson Letterbook.

74. UWI, John Whittaker to Long, Drake, Long & Dawkins, April 13, 1794, August 6, 1794, Gale-Morant Family Papers.

75. JA, Manumissions Liber, 1760–65, 1772, fol. 119, 1B/11/6/7; Hall, *In Miserable Slavery,* 314; Burnard, *Mastery, Tyranny, and Desire,* 229.

76. UWI, Thomas Thistlewood Diaries, August 24, 1761, Monson 31/12; Hall, *In Miserable Slavery,* 122. Thistlewood thought Coobah's child was either Mr. Cope's or that of Coobah's partner, Mulatto Davie. See Burnard, *Mastery, Tyranny, and Desire,* 234.

77. Nugent, *Lady Nugent's Journal,* 78.

78. NLJ, William Adlam to John Wemyss, February 1, 1820, Letterbook of John Wemyss.

79. Livesay, "The Decline of Jamaica's Interracial Households," 110.

80. The law went into effect in 1762. UWI, Journals of the Assembly of Jamaica, vol. 5, fol. 311, MR 3719. The Assembly, by a vote of nineteen to four, renewed this law in 1775. See JA, Laws of Jamaica, 16 George III, c. 14 (1775).

81. Long, *The History of Jamaica,* 2: 321–23; Phillippo, *Jamaica,* 60.

82. Gardner, *A History of Jamaica,* 172.

83. Livesay, "The Decline of Jamaica's Interracial Households," 110.

84. JA, Votes of the Assembly, 1810, fol. 130.

85. Livesay, "The Decline of Jamaica's Interracial Households," 111.

86. Ibid. Livesay argues that more than 80 percent of privileged Jamaicans received inheritance rights after 1761.

87. JA, Votes of the Assembly, 1787, fol. 105.

88. UWI, Journals of the Assembly of Jamaica, vol. 8, fol. 592, MR 3720.

89. IRO, Will of John Quier, Liber 103, fol. 7. Quier does not state what his relationship was to Catherine Ann Smith.

90. IRO, Will of Frances Mackie, Liber 106, fol. 164.

91. NLJ, *Postscript to the Royal Gazette*, November 20–27, 1813.

92. JA, Laws of Jamaica, 54 George III, c. 19 (1813).

93. Livesay, "The Decline of Jamaica's Interracial Households," 116.

94. Hall, *Civilising Subjects*, 79. Hall asserts that it was the crisis over abolition that forced the Jamaica Assembly to grant the same rights and privileges enjoyed by whites.

95. Moreton, *Manners and Customs*, 123.

96. Long, *The History of Jamaica*, 2: 261.

3 / "Train up a child"

1. Proverbs 22:6 quoted in NLJ, *Columbian Magazine* 2 (1798): 532, C652.

2. Foot, *A Defense of the Planters*, 100. The emphasis is Foot's.

3. See Elkins, *Slavery*; Stampp, *The Peculiar Institution*; Frazier, *Folk Beliefs of the Southern Negro*; Bastide, *African Civilisations in the New World*; Mintz and Price, *The Birth of African-American Culture*. Melville J. Herskovits was the only scholar at the time to disagree; see *The Myth of the Negro Past*.

4. See, for example, Holloway, *Africanisms in American Culture*; Chambers, "Ethnicity in the Diaspora"; Okpewho et al., *The African Diaspora*; Sweet, *Recreating Africa*; Konadu, *The Akan Diaspora*.

5. See Klein, "The English Slave Trade to Jamaica"; McDonald, "Measuring the British Slave Trade to Jamaica"; Burnard and Morgan, "The Dynamics of the Slave Market and Slave Purchasing Patterns in Jamaica"; Vasconcellos, "From Chattel to Breeding Wenches"; Diptee, *From Africa to Jamaica*. In 1789 the Assembly estimated that 25 percent of the enslaved population in Jamaica was African-born. Higman argues that this is a low estimate given the fact that 37 percent of the enslaved population on the island was African-born in 1817 (*Slave Population of Jamaica*, 75).

6. Higman, *Slave Population of Jamaica*, 76. Higman argues that the two main ethnic groups from these two regions were Ibo and Congo, respectively.

7. Equiano, *The Interesting Narrative*, 145.

8. Phillippo, *Jamaica*, 93.

9. Bisset, *The History of the Negro Slave Trade*, 1: 414. See also Kelly, *Jamaica in 1831*, 20–21; UWI, Thomas Thistlewood Diaries, Monson 31/1–31/35; Hall, *In Miserable Slavery*. For more on slave music and dance in the Caribbean, see Handler and Frisbie, "Aspects of Slave Life in Barbados"; Altink, "More than Producers and Reproducers"; Munro, "Slaves to the Rhythm."

10. Long, *The History of Jamaica*, 2: 142.

11. DU, Stephen Fuller to Henry Dundas, March 19, 1794, Stephen Fuller Papers.

12. Beckford, *Remarks Upon the Situation of Negroes in Jamaica*, 23.

13. Chambers, "Tracing Igbo into the African Diaspora," 65. See also Warner-Lewis, *Archibald Monteith*.

14. Warner-Lewis, "The Character of African-Jamaican Culture," 90. For more on slave naming practices, see DeCamp, "African Day-Names in Jamaica"; Handler and Jacoby, "Slave Names and Naming"; Burnard, "Slave Naming Patterns."

15. JA, May Smith Papers, 7/13/273. I have not been able to uncover an explanation as to why these particular days were considered lucky or unlucky. The focus on Monday could be a belief that developed in Jamaica, as the work assigned to each gang on Monday usually was performed for the remainder of the week.

16. Equiano, *Interesting Narrative*, 42. Equiano states that his name signifies fortune, or one who is favored with a loud voice and who is well spoken.

17. See JA, Registry of the Returns of Slaves, 1817, 1B/11/7.

18. See ibid. Occasionally bookkeepers differentiated among slaves with the same name by affixing numbers to their name, such as 1, 2, and 3 or 1st, 2nd, and 3rd. Others attached age to their names by calling them Old Sam and Young Sam or Old Bess and Young Bess.

19. NLJ, Radnor Plantation.

20. Lewis, *Journal of a West Indian Proprietor*, 219.

21. JA, Thetford Plantation Books, 4/23/9–11.

22. Burnard, "Slave Naming Patterns," 326.

23. JA, Registry of the Returns of Slaves, Westmoreland, 1B/11/7/9, St. George, 1B/11/7/22.

24. Moumouni, *Education in Africa*, 20–21. See also Omolewa, "Traditional African Modes of Education."

25. NLJ, "Jamaican Proverbs," Lily Perkins Collection; Senior, *A–Z of Jamaican Heritage*, 1.

26. Senior, *A–Z of Jamaican Heritage*, 1. Ackee and saltfish is the national dish of Jamaica.

27. NLJ, "Jamaican Proverbs," Lily Perkins Collection.

28. UWI, Thomas Thistlewood Diaries, May 16, 1751, Monson 31/2.

29. UWI, Thomas Thistlewood Diaries, May 16, 1751, Monson 31/2.

30. NLJ, "Anancy Stories," Lily Perkins Collection. Another story in this collection tells of a magical bag of yams found by Anansi one day in a distant field. Only Anansi knew the secret word that enabled the bag to produce more yams. Every night Anansi tortured his family by refusing them yams unless they could say the secret words. It was not until Anansi's son followed him one day and heard him speak the words that Anansi's family shared in his feast.

31. Lewis, *Journal of a West Indian Proprietor*, 155–58. For Anansi stories, see Beckwith, *Jamaica Anansi Stories*; Brathwaite, *The Development of Creole Society in Jamaica*; Purchas-Tulloch, "Jamaica Anansi"; Tanna, "Anansi"; Henry and Rowe, "Anansi Stories"; Auld, "Anansesem"; Tanna, *Jamaican Folk Tales and Oral Histories*; Tortello, "The Magical Spider-man"; De Souza, "Creolizing Anancy"; James, "From Orature to Literature"; Marshall, "Anansi, Eshu, and Legba"; Marshall, *Anansi's Journey*.

32. Marshall, *Anansi's Journey*, 4. Marshall also argues in her book that these stories encouraged and represented slave resistance and survival by warning against weakness, speaking against community issues and problems, and creating an outlet for satire and role reversal (4, 178).

33. NLJ, Mervyn Alleyne, "The Evolution of African Languages in Jamaica"; Senior, *A–Z of Jamaican Heritage*, 6.

34. We do have an idea of how these African cultural traditions were maintained and reinvented in Jamaica and the wider Caribbean. See Mullin, *Africa in America*; Buckridge, *The Language of Dress*; Aborampah, "Out of the Same Bowl"; Delle and Hauser, *Out of Many, One People*.

35. Chambers, "The Links of a Legacy," 287–88; NLJ, *Royal Gazette*, June 4–11, 1791.

36. For more on Jamaican patois, see Lalla and D'Costa, *Language in Exile*.

37. Cassidy and Le Page, *Dictionary of Jamaican English*, xli, xi. Silvia Kouwenberg does not discount that the Akan did have some influence on Jamaican patois but argues that it postdates this formative period and is more influenced by "the Gbe languages of the Bight of Benin, the Bantu languages of West Central Africa, and the Igbo and other languages of the Bight of Biafra" ("Africans in Early English Jamaica," 41).

38. Chambers, "'My own nation,'" 86.

39. Cassidy and Le Page, *Dictionary of Jamaican English*, 436. The actual Ewe word is *tálala*, meaning "direct, straightforward, thorough, to a high degree, entire, basic."

40. Long, *The History of Jamaica*, 2: 426–27.

41. Gardner, *A History of Jamaica*, 183; Renny, *An History of Jamaica*, 167. While Renny wrote his *History* in 1807, Gardner's *History of Jamaica* was published posthumously in 1874, not long after his death (Cundall, *Historic Jamaica*, 195).

42. Warner-Lewis, "The Character of African-Jamaican Culture," 91.

43. UWI, Thomas Thistlewood Diaries, June 19, 1765, Monson 31/16; Hall, *In Miserable Slavery*, 135.

44. Edwards, *History of Jamaica*, 152.

45. Acholonu, *The Igbo Roots of Olaudah Equiano*, 20, 29; Equiano, *Interesting Narrative*, 34–35.

46. UWI, Thomas Thistlewood Diaries, March 15, 1752, Monson 31/3.

47. Turner, *Slaves and Missionaries*, 11, 8. For more on missionaries in Jamaica and the greater Caribbean during this period, see Catron, "Across the Great Water"; Catron, "Evangelical Networks"; Dunkley, *Agency of the Enslaved*; Beasley, *Christian Ritual and the Creation of British Slave Societies*; Kenny, *Contentious Liberties*; Warner-Lewis, *Archibald Monteith*.

48. UWI, Journals of the Assembly of Jamaica, vol. 10, fols. 72–74, MR 3720; Wright, *Knibb, "the Notorious,"* 25.

49. JA, Laws of Jamaica, 8 George III, c. 16 (1807).

50. Waddell, *Twenty-nine Years*, 37.

51. Phillippo, *Jamaica*, 85, 96. Phillippo noted that once the enslaved population was Christianized, they lost many of their savage customs and no longer practiced polygamy or concubinage to the degree that they did as "savages" (90).

52. JA, Laws of Jamaica, 57 George III, c. 25 (1816).

53. JA, Votes of the Assembly, 1799–1800, fols. 25–26. See also a published extract of Parliamentary proceedings printed in NLJ, *Postscript to the Royal Gazette*, June 18–25, 1791. D. A. Dunkley argues that the Jamaican Assembly decided on a program to baptize the entire enslaved population of Jamaica in 1797 as part of the Assembly's amelioration policies. See Dunkley, *Agency of the Enslaved*, 121.

54. For more on Christian slave marriages and baptisms, see Turner, *Slaves and Missionaries*; Green, "'A Civil Inconvenience'?"; Beasley, *Christian Ritual and the Creation of British Slave Societies*.

55. JA, Register of Marriages, Kingston, fols. 165, 180 1B/11/8/8/14. Marriage registries do not survive for Jamaica's other parishes for these years. However, given that Kingston was an urban parish, it is likely that Christian marriage was more acceptable there than in the rural parishes. Not only were Kingston's slaves largely domestics, but their owners held different expectations for their moral well-being.

56. *A Short Review of the Slave Trade and Slavery*, 61; Higman, "The Slave Family and Household," 272.

57. Phillippo, *Jamaica*, 90. Phillippo further noted that the Christianization of the freedmen of the island had made the community respectable, moral, "graceful in manners, and social in disposition."

58. Turner, *Slaves and Missionaries*, 76.

59. Beasley, *Christian Ritual and the Creation of British Slave Societies*, 82.

60. Rose, *A Letter on the Means and Importance of Converting the Slaves*, 77.

61. See JA, Register of Baptisms, Marriages, Burials, St. Catherine (St. Dorothy and St. John), 1B/11/8/3/22; JA, Baptisms, Portland, 1B/11/8/12/1.

62. Dunkley, *Agency of the Enslaved*, 125. Archival sources suggest that by 1826 the entire Jamaican enslaved population was baptized. From that point on, slaves were baptized at their birth. See JA, Register of Baptisms, Marriages, Burials, St. Catherine (St. Dorothy and St. John), 1B/11/8/3/22; JA, Baptisms of Slaves, Hanover, 1B/11/8/7/1; JA, Baptisms, Manchester, 1B/11/8/10/3; JA, Baptisms, Portland, 1B/11/8/12/1; JA, Slave Baptisms, St. Ann, 1B/11/8/2/3.

63. De la Beche, *Notes on the Present Condition of the Negroes*, 27. In 1826 the Jamaican Assembly decreed that all slave baptisms were free of charge. See JA, Laws of Jamaica, 7 George IV, c. 23 (1826).

64. JA, Register of Baptisms, Marriages, Deaths, St. Thomas in the East, 1B/11/8/14/2.

65. JA, Register of Baptisms, Marriages, Burials, St. Catherine (St. Dorothy and St. John), IB/11/8/3/22; JA, Baptisms of Slaves, Hanover, 1B/11/8/7/1.

66. Bickell, *The West Indies as They Are*, 91.

67. Waddell, *Twenty-nine Years*, 23.

68. Lewis, *Journal of a West Indian Proprietor*, 80, 155–59, 253–61.

69. See JA, Registry of the Returns of Slaves, 1826, 1B/11/7/77–95. This is not to say that the slave community discontinued private use of these names. In the American South, for example, some enslaved children went by two names. While their owner approved one name, the other was a "basket name" known only to the other slaves. See Schwartz, *Born in Bondage*, 169; Gutman, *The Black Family in Slavery and Freedom*, 186, 576.

70. Lewis, *Journal of a West Indian Proprietor*, 78.

71. Yates, *Colonial Slavery*, 76.

72. Bridges, *The Annals of Jamaica*, 2: 430.

73. Hibbert, *Facts Verified Upon Oath*, 3. See also Rose, *A Letter on the Means and Importance of Converting the Slaves*, 52.

74. Bunn, *An Essay on the Abolition of Slavery*, 11–13.

75. For more on slave education in the Caribbean, see Blouet, "To Make Society Safe for Freedom."

76. Waddell, *Twenty-Nine Years*, 119.

77. It seems that this school was merely one part of a much larger program of reform. According to James Robertson, the Vestry already supported a School of Industry that taught a basic educational platform with religious instruction, alongside gender-specific tasks. Parish boys learned various skills and trades, such as tailor work, basket and hat making, cobbling, and cabinetry, while parish girls were taught sewing, straw weaving, and bonnet making. That school opened in 1826. Within four years the Vestry mandated the education of children belonging to anyone receiving parish aid under penalty of withheld aid. See Robertson, *Gone Is the Ancient Glory*, 155.

78. British Parliamentary Papers, "Jamaica: Religious Instruction," 329. It is likely that some children traveled from estate to estate on a weekly basis rather than taking up permanent residence on one particular estate.

79. *Marly*, 277.

80. It is important to note here that many planters blamed the missionaries for the increased rebelliousness of the slave community in the 1820s and 1830s. In fact most planters firmly believed that Baptist missionaries were the sole cause of the slave rebellions that devastated the island in 1831 and 1832. For more information on the relationship between Jamaican missionaries and Jamaican planters, as well as the relationship between these missionaries and the slave community, see Turner, *Slaves and Missionaries*; Matthews, *Caribbean Slave Revolts and the British Abolitionist Movement*; Dierksheide, "Missionaries, Evangelical Identity, and the Religious Ecology."

81. Legion, *A Second Letter*, 39.

82. Jackson, *A Memoir of Rev. John Jenkins*, 87.

83. British Parliamentary Papers, "Evidence of Rev. John Barry"; Great Britain, Parliament, House of Lords, *Abstract of the Report of the Lords Committees*, 34. Others agreed. See testimony from Sir George Rose, Reverend H. Jenkins of St. James, and Reverend T. P. Williams of Clarendon in *Substance of the Debate in the House of Commons*, 162.

4 / "That iniquitous law"

The title of this chapter comes from NLJ, Mr. Scott to Rowland Alston, July 24, 1834, Georgia Estate Letterbook.

1. JA, Votes of the Assembly, 1836–37, no. 1, fols. 144–45.

2. JA, Laws of Jamaica, 4 William IV, c. 33 (1833).

3. JA, Votes of the Assembly, 1836, fol. 29. It is important to note that the six-year apprenticeship period in Jamaica ended two years early, in 1838.

4. JA, Laws of Jamaica, 4 William IV, c. 33 (1833). Designed by an Englishman named Samuel Cubitt in 1818, the treadmill was a hollow cylinder of wood carved into a series of steps that sat on an iron frame. Wardens affixed a bar above the treadmill to which the apprentice's wrists were strapped. Once attached to the bar, the apprentices were forced to turn the wheel themselves by walking the steps for a set period of time. See Holt, *The Problem of Freedom*, 106. For treadmills, see Shayt, "Stairway to Redemption"; Turner, "The 11 O'Clock Flog"; Paton, *No Bond but the Law*. For workhouses in Jamaica, see Crowther, *The Workhouse System*; Altink, "Slavery by Another Name"; Newton, "Freedom's Prisons."

5. Butler, *The Economics of Emancipation*, 37. Nearly one third of the slave compensation fund was appropriated to Jamaican planters. See Hovey, *Letters from the West Indies*, 121–22.

6. *A Safe and Practical Course in the West India Question*, 7. See also, DU, Herbert J. James to James George Crabbe, April 24, 1834, James George Crabbe Papers.

7. Bunn, *An Essay on the Abolition of Slavery*, 15.

8. NLJ, Affidavits of Aggrieved Apprentices in Jamaica, Beldam Papers, MS 321a, no. 3.

9. JA, Records of Visitations, Adjudications, &c. by Special Justice Carnaby in St. James, January–June 1836, 1B/11/23/9. For other cases see JA, Votes of the Assembly, 1837–38, no. 1, fol. 59; Thome and Kimball, *Emancipation in the West Indies*, 107.

10. JA, Votes of the Assembly, 1837–38, no. 1, fol. 58.

11. *A Statement of Facts*, 7.

12. JA, Copy of a Letter from R. Cocking to W. G. Nunes, June 29, 1835, Votes of the Assembly, 1835, no. 2, fol. 179.

13. Sterne, *A Statement of Facts*, 254.

14. NLJ, Governor Sligo to T. S. Rice, August 24, 1834, Sligo Letterbook.

15. M'Mahon, *Jamaica Plantership*, 357.

16. JA, Votes of the Assembly, 1837–38, no. 1, fol. 58.

17. Ibid., Appendix 57, fol. 687, no. 3, fols. 63, 680.

18. Ibid., 1834, no. 3, fol. 670. See also the testimony of planter George Marrett, fol. 621.

19. Ibid., fol. 107. For more on the usage of indentured laborers in the postemancipation Caribbean, see Schuler, *"Alas, Alas, Kongo"*; Look Lai, *Indentured labor, Caribbean Sugar*; Shepherd, *Transients to Settlers*; Kale, *Fragments of Empire*; Wilson, *The Chinese in the Caribbean*; Brown, "Experiments in Indenture"; Drescher, *The Mighty Experiment*; Keating-Miller and Given, *Explorations of Affiliation*; Yun, *The Coolie Speaks*; Lutz, "Chinese Emigrants, Indentured Workers, and Christianity."

20. JA, Votes of the Assembly, 1836–37, no. 1, fol. 279. Of the forty-four from Liverpool, twenty-four were fifteen or younger. See also Senior, "The *Robert Kerr* Emigrants."

21. Hall, "The Apprenticeship System in Jamaica," 12.

22. UWI, Dr. John Rhodes Hulme, Circular 639, Jamaica Special Magistracy Papers. This circular makes clear that these children became apprentices, not indentured laborers. Therefore, Margaret Gilzean received approval from the children's mother.

23. JA, Votes of the Assembly, 1836, fols. 25–26.

24. Ibid., 1834, no. 3, fol. 63.

25. Ibid., 1835, no. 2, fol. 62.

26. JA, Mortgage Ledger, 7/257/1.

27. JA, Laws of Jamaica, 4 William IV, c. 33 (1833); Sterne, *A Statement of Facts*, 264.

28. Waddell, *Twenty-nine Years*, 118.

29. JA, Laws of Jamaica, 4 William IV, c. 33 (1833); Shepherd, "The Apprenticeship Experience," 49. It is unknown whether this ever happened in Jamaica. Strangely, planters never tried to force the issue with their laborers. Instead, they tried to convince their laborers to consent to the apprenticeship of free children on the island.

30. NLJ, John Salmon to J. G. Crabbe, September 16, 1836, Bouchier Correspondence.

31. JA, Report of John Cooper on Burrowfield Pen, April 18, 1835, John W. Cooper's Reports on the Properties of Simon Taylor, 7/177/1.

32. *Negro Apprenticeship in the Colonies*, 33.

33. Thome and Kimball, *Emancipation in the West Indies*, 102.

34. JA, Laws of Jamaica, 4 William IV, c. 33 (1833); JA, Votes of the Assembly, 1836, fol. 209. Not only was the number of hours per week reduced, but the terms of apprenticeship stipulated that Jamaica's apprentices only work four and a half days per week, the remaining time to be spent at their discretion. However, apprentices could choose to work extra hours for extra wages.

35. JA, Report of John Cooper on Lysson's Estate, April 18, 1835, John W. Cooper's Reports on the Properties of Simon Taylor, 7/177/2.

36. JA, Votes of the Assembly, 1834, no. 3, fols. 637, 650. McCornack and Gordon do not state whether children between the ages of six and fifteen performed extra work.

37. Ibid., 1836–37, no. 1, fol. 880.

38. JA, Report of John Cooper on Llanrumney Estate, April 18, 1835, John W. Cooper's Reports on the Properties of Simon Taylor, 7/177/6.

39. JA, Records of Visitations, Adjudications, &c. by Special Justice Carnaby in St. James, January–June 1836, 1B/11/23/9. Sukey states in her complaint that she is having difficulty keeping up the pace of the first gang.

40. NLJ, Affidavits of Aggrieved Apprentices in Jamaica, Beldam Papers, MS 321a, no. 3.

41. JA, Votes of the Assembly, 1834, no. 1, fol. 68.

42. *A Statement of Facts*, 11–12. The parish of the estate and workhouse is unknown.

43. Gardner, *A History of Jamaica*, 313.

44. JA, Governor Sligo to Thomas Spring Rice, August 13, 1834, Votes of the Assembly, 1835, no. 2, fol. 33.

45. Williams, *A Narrative of Events*(1837), 15. In her introduction to the reprint of Williams's *Narrative,* Diana Paton notes the complications of the account. Because he told his account to a white writer, the text is more of a collaborative effort that provides "evidence about the strategies and assumptions of those involved in the transatlantic campaign against apprenticeship" than a former slave's account of his life on a Jamaican estate. Interestingly, Paton recognizes Joseph Sturge, coauthor of *The West Indies in 1837,* as the driving force behind the narrative, as well as the person who facilitated the narrative's documentation and publication. See Williams, *Narrative of Events* (2001), xiv–xv.

46. JA, Votes of the Assembly, 1836–37, no 1, Appendix 4, fol. 426

47. Ibid. See also Appendix 47, fols. 829, 886.

48. Ibid., Appendix 4, fol. 426.

49. Ibid., fol. 156.

50. Sturge and Harvey, *The West Indies in 1837,* 217–18. Pryce's sentencing of the women to the workhouse would leave their provision grounds vulnerable to weeds and theft, concerns that also could have weighed heavily their minds during their time in the St. Ann Workhouse.

51. NLJ, Governor Sligo to Thomas Spring Rice, October 15, 1834, Sligo Letterbook.

52. JA, Votes of the Assembly, 1835, no. 2, fol. 90.

53. NLJ, *Kingston Chronicle*, August 16, 1834.

54. Waddell, *Twenty-nine Years*, 119.

55. JA, Votes of the Assembly, 1835, no. 2, fol. 169.

56. Winn, *Emancipation*, 34–35.

57. NLJ, "Extract from the Speech of the Marquis of Sligo to the Legislature of Jamaica," Working of the Apprenticeship System in the British Colonies; NLJ, *Royal Gazette*, April 4–11, 1835.

58. JA, Votes of the Assembly, 1836, fol. 79, 1836–37, no. 1, fol. 97.

59. Ibid., 1836, fol. 79.

60. Sturge and Harvey, *The West Indies in 1837,* 260. The parish of these two estates is unknown.

61. JA, Votes of the Assembly, 1834, no. 3, fol. 528.

62. NLJ, John Salmon to J. G. Crabbe, August 15, 1836, Bouchier Correspondence.

63. *Negro Apprenticeship in the Colonies*, 34; NLJ, "Extract from the Speech of the Marquis of Sligo to the Legislature of Jamaica," Working of the Apprenticeship System in the British Colonies. The emphasis is Sligo's.

64. Latrobe, *Copy of a Report*, 5–11.

65. Martin, *Statistics of the Colonies*, 8, 10.

66. Phillippo, *Jamaica*, 69.

Conclusions

1. For more on these stages of childhood, see Ariès, *Centuries of Childhood*; Plumb, "The New World of Children"; Zelizer, *Pricing the Priceless Child*; Pollack, *A Lasting Relationship*; Archard, *Children*; Heywood, *A History of Childhood*.

References

Archives

Island Record Office, Spanish Town, Jamaica

Will of John Quier, 1819
Will of Frances Mackie, 1826

Jamaica Archives, Spanish Town, Jamaica

Baptisms of Slaves, Hanover, 1817–34, 1B/11/8/7
Baptisms, Manchester, 1827–33, 1B/11/8/10
Baptisms, Portland, 1804–26, 1B/11/8/12
Braco Estate, 1795–97, 4/2
Committee of Correspondence, Letterbook from Agents in London, S. Fuller and R. Sewell, 1795–1801, 1B/4
John W. Cooper's Reports on the Properties of Simon Taylor, 1835, 7/177
Dispatches, England to Jamaica, 1800–1830, 1B/5
Green Park Estate, 1821–31, 4/8
Harmony Hall Estate, 1796–1832, 7/56
Journal of Benjamin Scott Moncrieffe, 1825–40, 1A/5
Kelly Family Papers, 4/43
Laws of Jamaica, 1735–1838
Manumissions Liber, 1750–1834, 1B/11/6
May Smith Papers, 7/13
Mortgage Ledger, 1835–70, 7/257
Port Royal Summary Slave Trials, 1819–34, 2/19
Records of Visitations, Adjudications, &c. by Special Justice Carnaby in St. James, 1836, 1B/11/23

Register of Baptisms, Marriages, Burials, St. Catherine (St. Dorothy and St. John), 1693–1836, 1B/11/8/3
Register of Baptisms, Marriages, Deaths, St. Thomas in the East, 1817–25, 1B/11/8/14
Register of Marriages, Kingston, 1753–1814, 1B/11/8/8
Registry of the Returns of Slaves, 1817–34, 1B/11/7
Rose Hall Estate, 1817–22, 1B/26
Slave Baptisms, St. Ann, 1817–26, 1B/11/8/2
Thetford Plantation Books, 1798–1833, 4/23
Tweedie Family Papers, 4/45
Votes of the Assembly, 1750–1838
Worthy Park Estate, 1791–1834, 4/23

National Library of Jamaica, Kingston, Jamaica

Mervyn Alleyne, "The Evolution of African Languages in Jamaica," unpublished manuscript, MS 2027
The Beldam Papers, MS 321
The Bouchier Correspondence, 1836–37, MS 377
Carlton Estate, 1810–16, MS 131
Columbian Magazine
Duke of Manchester Accounts, 1823–27, MS 1768
Roger Hope Elletson Letterbook, 1773–80, MS 29
Georgia Estate Letterbook, 1805–35, MS 132
Gray Correspondence, 1809–18, MS 163
Harmony Hall Estate, 1818–24, MS 1652
Jamaica Journal
Kingston Chronicle
Maryland Estate, 1817–25, MS 355
Moorshall Estate, 1813–14, MS 2008
Lily Perkins Collection, MS 2019
Sligo Letterbook, 1834–36, MS 281
St. Ann Slave Court, 1787–1814, MS 273
Postscript to the Royal Gazette (Kingston)
Radnor Plantation, 1822–26, MS 180
Royal Gazette (Kingston)
Somerset Plantation, 1782–96
Spring Vale Journal and Accounts, 1790–1815, MS 236
Letterbook of John Wemyss, 1819–24, MS 250
Working of the Apprenticeship System in the British Colonies, 1836, MS 1887

West India Collection, University of the West Indies, Mona, Jamaica

Dickenson Family Papers, 1675–1849, MR 515, MR 518, MR 2599–600, MR 2950–53

Gale-Morant Family Papers, 1731–1925, MR 769
Dr. John Rhodes Hulme, Jamaica Special Magistracy Papers, MR 420
Journals of the Assembly of Jamaica, 1750–1820, MR 3719–21
Penrhyn Castle Papers, 1709–1834, MS 1361
Slebach Collection, MR 527–29, MR 541, MR 543
Stowe Collection, MR 509
Thomas Thistlewood Diaries, 1750–86, Monson 31/1–31/31

William L. Clements Library, University of Michigan, Ann Arbor, Michigan

Memoir of Charles Machin, 1807–20
James Stothert Papers, 1787–1807

Duke University Special Collections Library, Durham, North Carolina

James George Crabbe Papers, 1823–34
Stephen Fuller Papers, 1702–98

British Parliamentary Papers

"Jamaica: Religious Instruction: Reports Concerning Religious Instruction of Coloured and Enslaved population and Number of Churches in Jamaica" (no. 481), 1831–32, 47: 323–29.

"Evidence of Rev. John Barry," in "Report from the Select Committee on the Extinction of Slavery Throughout the British Dominions: with the Minutes of Evidence" (no. 721), 1831–32, 20: 68.

"Evidence of Robert Hibbert," in "Minutes, &c. Reported To The House, Veneris, 19° die Martii 1790" (no. 72), 1790, 87: 360–69.

Printed Primary Sources

Beckford, William. *A Descriptive Account of the Island of Jamaica: With Remarks upon the Cultivation of the Sugar-Cane, throughout the different Seasons of the Year, and Chiefly Considered in a Picturesque Point of View; also Observations and Reflections upon What would Probably be the Consequences of an Abolition of the Slave-Trade, and the Emancipation of the Slaves.* Vol. 2. London: T. and J. Egerton, 1790.

———. *Remarks Upon the Situation of Negroes in Jamaica, Impartially Made from a Local Experience of Nearly Thirteen Years in that Island.* London: T. and J. Egerton, 1788.

Bickell, Richard. *The West Indies as They Are; or a Real Picture of Slavery: But More Particularly as It Exists in the Island of Jamaica.* London: J. Hatchard and Son, 1825.

Bisset, Robert. *The History of the Negro Slave Trade, in its Connection with the Commerce and Prosperity of the West Indies, and the Wealth and Power of the British Empire.* 2 vols. London: W. McDowall, 1805.

Bridges, George Wilson. *The Annals of Jamaica*. 2 vols. London: J. Murray, 1828.

Bunn, T. *An Essay on the Abolition of Slavery Throughout the British Dominions, Without Injury to the Master or His Property, With the Least Possible Injury to the Slave, Without Revolution, and Without Loss to the Revenue*. Frome, UK: W. P. Penny, 1833.

Dr. Collins. *Practical Rules for the Management and Medical Treatment of Negro Slaves, in the Sugar Colonies*. London: J. Barfield, 1811.

Cooper, Thomas. *Facts Illustrative of the Condition of the Negro Slaves in Jamaica*. London: G. Smallfield, 1824.

Corry, Joseph. *Observations Upon the Windward Coast of Africa, the Religion, Character, Customs, &c. of the Natives, With a System Upon Which They May Be Civilized and a Knowledge Attained of the Interior of this Extraordinary Quarter of the Globe and Upon the Natural and Commercial Resources of the Country, Made in the Years 1805 and 1806*. London: G. and W. Nicol, 1807. Reprint, London: Frank Cass, 1968.

Dancer, Thomas. *The Medical Assistant, or, Jamaica Practice of Physic: Designed Chiefly for the Use of Families and Plantations*. London: Printed for R. Gilbert, 1819.

Davis, Anthony. *The West Indies*. London: N.p., 1832.

De la Beche, Henry. *Notes on the Present Condition of the Negroes in Jamaica*. London: T. Cadell, 1825.

Edwards, Bryan. *The History, Civil and Commercial, of the British Colonies in the West Indies in Two Volumes*. Vol. 2. London: John Stockdale, 1793.

Equiano, Olaudah. *The Interesting Narrative of the Life of Olaudah Equiano, Written by Himself*. Edited by Robert J. Allison. New York: W. Durell, 1791. Reprint, Boston: Bedford Books, 1995.

Flügel, George Thomas, and Francis Joseph Grund. *The Merchant's Assistant, or Mercantile Instructer: A Full Account of the Moneys, Coins, Weights and Measures of the Principle Trading Nations and Their Colonies; Together with Their Values in United States Currency, Weights and Measures*. Boston: Hilliard, Gray, 1834.

Foot, Jesse. *A Defense of the Planters of the West Indies*. London: J. Debrett, 1792.

Fuller, Stephen. *Notes on the Two Reports from the Committee of the Honourable House of Assembly on the Subject of the Slave-Trade*. London: B. White and Son, 1789.

———. *Report, Resolutions, and Remonstrance, of the Honourable The Council and Assembly of Jamaica, At a Joint Committee, on the Subject of the Slave-Trade, In a Session Which Began the 20th of October 1789*. London: B. White and Son, 1790.

Gardner, W. J. *A History of Jamaica from Its Discovery by Christopher Columbus to the Year 1872*. London: Elliot Stock, 1873. Reprint, London: Frank Cass, 1971.

Great Britain. Parliament. Agency Anti-Slavery Committee. *The Condition of the Slave, Not Preferable to That of the British Peasant, from the Evidence Before the Parliamentary Committees on Colonial Slavery.* London: W. Johnston, 1833.

———. Parliament. House of Commons. *House of Commons Sessional Papers of the Eighteenth Century.* Edited by Sheila Lambert. Vol. 68. Wilmington, DE: Scholarly Resources, 1975.

———. Parliament. House of Lords. *Abstract of the Report of the Lords Committees on the Condition and Treatment of the Colonial Slaves, and of the Evidence Taken by Them on that Subject.* London: Printed for the Society for the Abolition of Slavery Throughout the British Dominions, 1833.

Hibbert, Robert. *Facts Verified Upon Oath, in Contradiction of the Report of the Rev. Thomas Cooper, Concerning the General Condition of the Slaves in Jamaica.* London: John Murray, 1824.

Hinton, John, ed. *Memoir of William Knibb, Missionary to Jamaica.* London: Houlston and Stoneman, 1849.

Hovey, Sylvester. *Letters from the West Indies.* New York: Gould and Newman, 1838.

Jackson, George. *A Memoir of Rev. John Jenkins, Late a Wesleyan Missionary in the Island of Jamaica.* London: N.p., 1832.

Jamaica. House of Assembly. *An Act for the Better Order and Government of Slaves; and for Other Purposes.* St. Jago de la Vega, Jamaica: Alexander Aikman, 1801.

———. *The New Consolidated Act.* London: Printed for Stephen Fuller, Esq., 1789.

Kelly, James. *Jamaica in 1831: Being a Narrative of Seventeen Years' Residence in that Island.* Belfast: James Wilson, 1838.

Laborie, P. J. *The Coffee Planter of Saint Domingo.* London: T. Caddell and W. Davies, 1798.

Latrobe, C. J. *Copy of a Report from C. J. Latrobe, Esq., on Negro Education in Jamaica, with Correspondence Relating Thereto.* London: Printed for the House of Commons, 1838.

Legion. *A Second Letter from Legion to His Grace the Duke of Richmond.* London: S. Bagster, 1833.

Lewis, Matthew. *Journal of a West Indian Proprietor Kept During a Residence in the Island of Jamaica.* Edited by Judith Terry. London: John Murray, 1834. Reprint, Oxford: Oxford University Press, 1999.

Long, Edward. *The History of Jamaica, or, A General Survey of the Antient and Modern State of that Island.* 3 vols. London: T. Lowndes, 1770.

Madden, R. R. *Twelvemonths Residence in the West Indies.* London: James Cochrane, 1835.

Marly; or, the Life of a Planter in Jamaica: Comprehending Characteristic Sketches of the Present State of Society and Manners in the British West Indies and an Impartial Review of the Leading Questions Relative to Colonial Policy. 2nd edition. Glasgow: Richard Griffin, 1828.

Marsden, Peter. *An Account of the Island of Jamaica; with Reflections on the Treatment, Occupation, and Provisions of the Slaves*. London: N.p., 1788.

Martin, Robert Montgomery. *Statistics of the Colonies of the British Empire in the West Indies, South America, North America, Asia, Austral-Asia, Africa, and Europe*. London: William H. Allen, 1839.

Mathison, Gilbert. *Notices Respecting Jamaica, in 1808–1809–1810*. London: S. Gosnell, 1811.

M'Mahon, Benjamin. *Jamaica Plantership*. London: Effingham Wilson, 1839.

M'Neill, Hector. *Observations on the Treatment of the Negroes, in the Island of Jamaica*. London: G. G. J. and J. Robinson, 1788.

Moreton, J. B. *Manners and Customs in the West India Islands*. London: W. Richardson, 1790.

Negro Apprenticeship in the Colonies: A Review of the Report of the Select Committee of the House of Commons, Appointed to Inquire Into "The Working of the Apprenticeship System in the Colonies, the Condition of the Apprentices, and the Laws and Regulations Affecting Them Which Have Been Passed." London: John Hatchard and Son, 1837.

Nugent, Maria. *Lady Nugent's Journal*. Edited by Philip Wright. London: Issued for Private Circulation, 1839. Reprint, Kingston: University of the West Indies Press, 2002.

Perkins, Cyrus Francis. *Busha's Mistress or Catherine The Fugitive: A Stirring Romance of the Days of Slavery in Jamaica*. Edited by Paul E. Lovejoy, Verene A. Shepherd, and David V. Trotman. Kingston, Jamaica: Ian Randle, 2003.

Phillippo, James Mursell. *Jamaica: Its Past and Present State*. Philadelphia: James M. Campbell, 1848.

Pinkard, George. *Notes on the West Indies: Written During the Expedition Under the Command of the Late General Sir Ralph Abercromby*. Vol. 1. London: Longman, Hurst, Rees, and Orme, 1806. Reprint, Westport, CT: Negro Universities Press, 1970.

Ramsay, James. *An Essay on the Treatment and Conversion of African Slaves in the British Sugar Colonies*. London: James Phillips, 1784.

Reasons for Establishing a Registry of Slaves in the British Colonies. London: N.p., 1814.

Renny, Robert. *An History of Jamaica*. London: J. Cawthorn, 1807.

A Review of the Reasons Given for Establishing a Registry of Slaves in the British Colonies. London: Hachard, 1816.

Riland, John. *Memoirs of a West Indian Planter*. London: Hamilton, Adams, 1827.

Rose, Henry. *A Letter on the Means and Importance of Converting the Slaves in the West Indies to Christianity*. London: John Murray, 1823.

Roughly, Thomas. *The Jamaica Planter's Guide; or, a System for Planting and Managing a Sugar Estate, or Other Plantations in that Island, and Through-*

out the British West Indies in General. London: Longman, Hurst, Rees, Orme, and Brown, 1823.

A Safe and Practical Course in the West India Question. London: Maurice, 1833.

Sells, William. *Remarks on the Condition of the Slaves in the Island of Jamaica*. London: Hughes, 1825.

A Short Review of the Slave Trade and Slavery, with Considerations on the Benefit Which Would Arise from Cultivating Tropical Productions by Free Labour. Birmingham, UK: Beilby, Knott, and Beilby, 1827.

"The Slave Mother's Address." In *Five Slave Narratives: A Compendium*, edited by William Loren Katz. New York: Arno Press, 1968.

A Speech Delivered at a Free Conference Between the Honourable, the Council and Assembly of Jamaica: Held the 19th November, 1789, on the Subject of Mr. Wilberforce's Propositions in the House of Commons, Concerning the Slave-Trade. London: Printed for J. Debritt, 1790.

The Speech of Sir William Young, Bart. Delivered in Parliament on the Subject of the Slave Trade. London: John Stockdale, 1791.

A Statement of Facts Illustrating the Administration of the Abolition Law, and the Sufferings of the Negro Apprentices in the Island of Jamaica. London: John Haddon, 1837.

Sterne, Henry. *A Statement of Facts, Submitted to the Right Honorable Lord Glenelg*. London: J. C. Chappell, 1837. Reprint, New York: Negro Universities Press, 1969.

Stewart, John. *An Account of Jamaica and Its Inhabitants*. London: Longman, Hurst, Rees, and Orme, 1808. Reprint, Freeport, NY: Books for Libraries Press, 1971.

———. *A View of the Past and Present State of the Island of Jamaica with Remarks on the Moral and Physical Condition of the Slaves, and on the Abolition of Slavery in the Colonies*. London: Oliver and Boyd, 1823. Reprint, New York: Negro Universities Press, 1969.

Sturge, Joseph, and Thomas Harvey. *The West Indies in 1837*. London: Hamilton, Adams, 1838.

Substance of the Debate in the House of Commons, on the 15th May, 1823, on a Motion for the Mitigation and Gradual Abolition of Slavery Throughout the British Dominions. London: Ellerton and Henderson, 1823.

Thome, Thomas A., and Horace Kimball. *Emancipation in the West Indies*. New York: American Anti-Slavery Society, 1838.

Trelawny, Edward. *An Essay Concerning Slavery, and the Danger Jamaica Is Expos'd to from the Too Great Number of Slaves, and the Too Little Care that is Taken to Manage Them, and a Proposal to Prevent the Further Importation of Negroes into that Island*. London: Charles Corbett, 1745.

Waddell, Hope Masterton. *Twenty-nine Years in the West Indies and Central Africa, 1829–1858*. London: Nelson, 1863.

Williams, Cynric. *A Tour Through the Island of Jamaica, From the Western to the Eastern End, in the Year 1823*. 2nd edition. London: Thomas Hurst, Edward, 1827.

Williams, James. *A Narrative of Events Since the First of August, 1834*. London: J. Rider, 1837.

———. *A Narrative of Events Since the First of August, 1834, by James Williams, an Apprenticed Labourer in Jamaica*. Edited by Diana Paton. Durham, NC: Duke University Press, 2001.

Williamson, John. *Medical and Miscellaneous Observations, Relative to the West Indian Islands*. Vol. 1. Edinburgh: Printed by A. Smellie for the Author, 1817.

Winn, T. S. *Emancipation; or Practical Advice to British Slave-Holders: With Suggestions for the General Improvement of West India Affairs*. London: J. Cowell, 1824.

Yates, John Ashton. *Colonial Slavery: Letters to the Right Honorable William Huskisson*. Liverpool: Harris, 1824.

Published Secondary Sources

Aborampah, Osei-Mensah. "Out of the Same Bowl: Religious Beliefs and Practices in Akan Communities in Ghana and Jamaica." In *Fragments of Bone: Neo-African Religions in a New World*, edited by Patrick Bellgarde-Smith, 124–42. Champagne: University of Illinois Press, 2005.

Acholonu, Catherine Obianuju. *The Igbo Roots of Olaudah Equiano*. Owerri, Nigeria: AFA Publications, 1989.

Alleyne, Mervyn. *The Construction and Representation of Race and Ethnicity in the Caribbean and the World*. Mona: University of the West Indies Press, 2002.

———. *Roots of Jamaican Culture*. London: Pluto Press, 1989.

Altink, Henrice. "Forbidden Fruit: Pro-Slavery Attitudes towards Slave Women's Sexuality and Interracial Sex." *Journal of Caribbean History* 39 (2005): 201–35.

———. "'I Did Not Want to Face the Shame of Exposure': Gender Ideologies and Child Murder in Post-Emancipation Jamaica." *Journal of Social History* 41 (2007): 355–87.

———. "More than Producers and Reproducers: Jamaican Slave Women's Dance and Song in the 1770s-1830s." *Society for Caribbean Studies Annual Conference Papers* 1 (2000): n.p.

———. *Representations of Slave Women in Discourses on Slavery and Abolition, 1780–1838*. New York: Routledge, 2007.

———. "Slavery by Another Name: Apprenticed Women in Jamaican Workhouses in the Period, 1834–8." *Social History* 26 (2001): 40–59.

Anstey, Roger. "Capitalism and Slavery: A Critique." *Economic History Review* 21 (1968): 307–20.

Apprenticeship and Emancipation. Mona: Department of Extra-Mural Studies, University of the West Indies, 1970.

Archard, David. *Children: Rights and Childhood.* London: Routledge, 1993.

Ariès, Philippe. *Centuries of Childhood.* Translated by Robert Baldick. New York: Vintage Books, 1962.

Armstrong, Douglas V. "Afro-Jamaican Plantation Life: An Archaeological Study of Drax Hall." *Jamaica Journal* 24 (1991): 3–8.

———. *The Old Village and the Great House: An Archeological and Historical Investigation of Drax Hall Plantation, St. Ann's Bay, Jamaica.* Urbana: University of Illinois Press, 1990.

Auld, Michael. "Anansesem." *Jamaica Journal* 16 (1983): 35–36.

Barrett, Leonard E. *The Sun and the Drum: African Roots in Jamaican Folk Tradition.* Kingston, Jamaica: Sangster's Book Stores, 1976.

Bastide, Roger. *African Civilisations in the New World.* Translated by Peter Green. New York: Harper & Row, 1971.

Beasley, Nicholas M. *Christian Ritual and the Creation of British Slave Societies, 1650–1780.* Athens: University of Georgia Press, 2010.

Beckles, Hilary McD. *Centering Woman: Gender Discourses in Caribbean Slave Society.* Kingston, Jamaica: Ian Randle, 1999.

———. "Creolisation in Action: The Slave Labour Elite and Anti-Slavery in Barbados." *Caribbean Quarterly* 44 (1998): 108–28.

———. *Natural Rebels: A Social History of Enslaved Black Women in Barbados.* New Brunswick, NJ: Rutgers University Press, 1989.

Beckles Hilary McD., and Verene Shepherd. *Freedoms One: Caribbean Emancipations, Ethnicities and Nationhood.* Cambridge, UK: Cambridge University Press, 2007.

Beckwith, Martha Warren. *Black Roadways: A Study of Jamaican Folk Life.* New York: Negro Universities Press, 1969.

———. *Jamaica Anansi Stories.* New York: American Folk-lore Society, 1924.

———. *Jamaica Folk-lore.* New York: American Folk-lore Society, 1928.

Bender, Thomas, ed. *The Anti-Slavery Debate: Capitalism and Abolition as a Problem in Historical Interpretation.* Berkeley: University of California Press, 1992.

Besson, Jean. "The Creolization of African-American Slave Kinship in Jamaican Free Villages and Maroon Communities." In *Slave Cultures and the Culture of Slavery,* edited by Stephen Palmié, 187–209. Knoxville: University of Tennessee Press, 1995.

———. "Euro-Creole, Afro-Creole, Meso-Creole: Creolization and Ethnic Identity in West-Central Jamaica." In *A Pepper-Pot of Cultures: Aspects of Creolization in the Caribbean,* edited by Gordon Collier and Ulrich Fleischmann, 169–88. Amsterdam: Editions Rodopi, 2003.

Bilby, Kenneth, and Jerome Handler. "Obeah: Healing and Protection in West Indian Slave Life." *Journal of Caribbean History* 38 (2004): 153–83.

Blake, Beverley. "The Child on the Radnor Plantation, Jamaica, 1817–1832." Unpublished manuscript, University of the West Indies–Mona, 1987.

———. "A History of Children in Nineteenth Century Jamaica." M.Phil. thesis, University of the West Indies–Mona, 1990.

Blouet, Olwyn M. "To Make Society Safe for Freedom: Slave Education in Barbados, 1823–33." *Journal of Negro History* 65 (1980): 126–34.

Boulukos, George. *The Grateful Slave: The Emergence of Race in Eighteenth-Century British and American Culture*. Cambridge, UK: Cambridge University Press, 2008.

Brana-Shute, Rosemary, and Randy J. Sparks, eds. *Paths to Freedom: Manumission in the Atlantic World*. Columbia: University of South Carolina Press, 2009.

Brandenstein, C. "'Making "the agreeable" to the big wigs': Lady Nugent's Grand Tour of Jamaica, 1801–1805." In *In Transit: Travel, Text, Empire*, edited by Helen Gilbert and Anna Johnston, 45–64. New York: Peter Lang, 2002.

Brathwaite, Edward. *The Development of Creole Society in Jamaica, 1770–1820*. Oxford: Clarendon Press, 1971.

———. *The Folk Culture of the Slaves in Jamaica*. London: New Beacon Books, 1970.

Brown, Laurence. "Experiments in Indenture: Barbados and the Segmentation of Migrant Labor in the Caribbean, 1863–1865." *New West Indian Guide* 79 (2005): 31–54.

Brown, Vincent. *The Reaper's Garden: Death and Power in the World of Atlantic Slavery*. Cambridge, MA: Harvard University Press, 2008.

Buckridge, Steve O. *The Language of Dress: Resistance and Accommodation in Jamaica, 1750–1890*. Kingston: University of the West Indies Press, 2004.

Burn, W. L. *Emancipation and Apprenticeship in the British West Indies*. London: J. Cape, 1937.

Burnard, Trevor. "'The Countrie Continues Sicklie': White Mortality in Jamaica, 1655–1780." *Social History of Medicine* 12 (1999): 45–72.

———. "The Curious Decline of Jamaican Sugar Planters in the Foundational Period of British Abolitionism." *Slavery & Abolition* 32 (2011): 185–98.

———. "E Pluribus Plures: African Ethnicities in Seventeenth and Eighteenth Century Jamaica." *Jamaican Historical Review* 21 (2001): 8–22, 56–59.

———. "European Migration to Jamaica, 1655–1780." *William and Mary Quarterly* 53 (1996): 769–96.

———. "A Failed Settler Society: Marriage and Demographic Failure in Early Jamaica." *Journal of Social History* 28 (1994): 63–82.

———. *Mastery, Tyranny, and Desire: The Anglo-Jamaican World of Thomas Thistlewood and His Slaves, 1750–1786*. Mona: University of the West Indies Press, 2004.

———. "Passengers Only: The Extent and Significance of Absenteeism in Eighteenth Century Jamaica." *Atlantic Studies* 1 (2004): 178–95.

———. "'Prodigious Riches': The Wealth of Jamaica before the American Revolution." *Economic History Review* 54 (2001): 506–24.

———. "The Sexual Life of an Eighteenth Century Jamaican Slave Overseer." In *Sex and Sexuality in Early America*, edited by Merril D. Smith, 163–89. New York: New York University Press, 1998.

———. "Slave Naming Patterns: Onomastics and the Taxonomy of Race in Eighteenth-Century Jamaica." *Journal of Interdisciplinary History* 31 (2001): 325–46.

Burnard, Trevor, and Kenneth Morgan. "The Dynamics of the Slave Market and Slave Purchasing Patterns in Jamaica, 1655–1788." *William and Mary Quarterly* 58 (2001): 205–28.

Burton, Richard D. E. *Afro-Creole: Power, Opposition, and Play in the Caribbean*. Ithaca, NY: Cornell University Press, 1997.

Bush, Barbara. "Hard Labor: Women, Childbirth, and Resistance in British Slave Societies." In *More than Chattel: Black Women and Slavery in the Americas*, edited by David Barry Gaspar and Darlene Clark Hine, 194–217. Bloomington: Indiana University Press, 1996.

———. *Slave Women in Caribbean Society, 1650–1838*. Kingston, Jamaica: Heinemann, 1990.

Butler, Kathleen Mary. *The Economics of Emancipation: Jamaica and Barbados, 1823–1843*. Chapel Hill: University of North Carolina Press, 1995.

Campbell, C. "Social and Economic Obstacles to the Development of Popular Education in Post-Emancipation Jamaica, 1834–1865." *Journal of Caribbean History* 1 (1970): 57–88.

Campbell, John F. "How Free Is Free? The Limits of Manumission for African Slaves in Eighteenth-Century British West Indian Sugar Society." In *Paths to Freedom: Manumission in the Atlantic World*, edited by Rosemary Brana-Shute and Randy J. Sparks, 143–59. Columbia: University of South Carolina Press, 2009.

Carrington, Selwyn H. H. "Capitalism and Slavery and Caribbean Historiography: An Evaluation." *Journal of African American History* 88 (2003): 304–12.

Carrington, Selwyn H. H., and Seymour Drescher, "Debate: Econocide and West Indian Decline, 1783–1806." *Boletin de Estudios Latinoamericanos y del Caribe* 36 (1984): 13–67.

Cassidy, F. G., and R. B. Le Page. *Dictionary of Jamaican English*. 2nd edition. Mona: University of the West Indies Press, 2002.

Cateau, Heather, and S. H. H. Carrington, eds. *Capitalism and Slavery Fifty Year's Later: Eric Eustace Williams—A Reassessment of the Man and His Work*. New York: Peter Lang, 2000.

Catron, John W. "Across the Great Water: Religion and Diaspora in the Black Atlantic." Ph.D. Dissertation, University of Florida, 2008.

———. "Evangelical Networks in the Greater Caribbean and the Origins of the Black Church." *Church History* 79 (2010): 77–114.

Chambers, Douglas B. "Ethnicity in the Diaspora: The Slave-Trade and the Creation of African 'Nations' in the Americas." *Slavery & Abolition* 22 (2001): 25–39.

———. "The Links of a Legacy: Figuring the Slave Trade to Jamaica." In *Caribbean Culture: Soundings on Kamau Brathwaite*, edited by Annie Paul, 287–312. Kingston: University of the West Indies Press, 2007.

———. "'My own nation': Igbo Exiles in the Diaspora." In *Routes to Slavery: Direction, Ethnicity and Mortality in the Transatlantic Slave Trade*, edited by David Eltis and David Richardson, 72–97. London: Frank Cass, 1997.

———. "Tracing Igbo into the African Diaspora." In *Identity in the Shadow of Slavery*, edited by Paul E. Lovejoy, 55–71. London: Continuum, 2000.

Clarke, Colin. *Decolonizing the Colonial City: Urbanization and Stratification in Kingston, Jamaica*. Oxford: Oxford University Press, 2006.

Clover, David. "'This horably wicked action': Abortion and Resistance on a Jamaican Slave Plantation." *Society for Caribbean Studies Annual Conference Papers* 9 (2008): n.p.

Coclanis, Peter A. "The Wealth of British America on the Eve of the Revolution." *Journal of Interdisciplinary History* 21 (1990): 245–60.

Coelho, P. R. P., and R. A. McGuire. "Diets versus Diseases: The Anthropometries of Enslaved Children." *Journal of Economic History* 60 (2000): 232–46.

Crahan, Margaret E., and Franklin W. Knight, eds. *Africa and the Caribbean: The Legacies of a Link*. Baltimore: Johns Hopkins University Press, 1979.

Craton, Michael. "Changing Patterns of Slave Families in the British West Indies." *Journal of Interdisciplinary History* 10 (1979): 1–35.

———. "Death, Disease and Medicine on Jamaican Slave Plantations: The Example of Worthy Park, 1767–1838." *Histoire Sociale* 9 (1976): 237–55.

———. *Empire, Enslavement, and Freedom in the Caribbean*. Kingston, Jamaica: Ian Randle, 1997.

———. "Jamaican Slave Mortality: Fresh Light from Worthy Park, Longville and the Tharp Estates." *Journal of Caribbean History* 3 (1971): 1–27.

———. "The Oldest Jamaican Sugar Estate." *Jamaican Journal* 4 (1970): 2–4.

———. *Searching for the Invisible Man: Slaves and Plantation Life in Jamaica*. Cambridge, MA: Harvard University Press, 1978.

Craton, Michael, and James Walvin. *A Jamaican Plantation: A History of Worthy Park, 1670–1970*. London: W. H. Allen, 1970.

Crowther, M. A. *The Workhouse System, 1834–1929: The History of an English Social Institution*. Athens: University of Georgia Press, 1982.

Cundall, Frank. *Historic Jamaica: With Fifty-Two Illustrations*. London: Published for the Institute of Jamaica for the West India Committee, 1924.

Curtin, Philip. *The Atlantic Slave Trade: A Census*. Madison: University of Wisconsin Press, 1969.

Cutler, David, Angus Denton, and Adriana Lleras-Muney. "The Determinates of Mortality." *Journal of Economic Perspectives* 20 (2006): 97–120.

De Barros, Juanita. "'Setting Things Right': Medicine and Magic in British Guiana, 1803–38." *Slavery & Abolition* 25 (2004): 28–50.

DeCamp, David. "African Day-Names in Jamaica." *Language* (1967): 139–49.

Delle James A., and Mark W. Hauser, eds. *Out of Many, One People: The Historical Archaeology of Colonial Jamaica*. Birmingham: University of Alabama Press, 2011.

De Souza, P. "Creolizing Anancy: Signifyin(g) Processes in New World Spider Tales." *Matatu* 27 (2003): 339–66.

Dierksheide, Christa. "Missionaries, Evangelical Identity, and the Religious Ecology of Early Nineteenth-Century South Carolina and the British Caribbean." *American Nineteenth Century History* 7 (2006): 63–88.

Diptee, Audra. *From Africa to Jamaica: The Making of an Atlantic Slave Society, 1755–1807*. Gainesville: University Press of Florida, 2010.

Draper, Nicholas. *The Price of Emancipation: Slave-Ownership, Compensation and British Society at the End of Slavery*. Cambridge, UK: Cambridge University Press, 2010.

Drescher, Seymour. *Capitalism and Antislavery: British Mobilization in Comparative Perspective*. Oxford: Oxford University Press, 1986.

———. "The Decline Thesis of British Slavery since Econocide." *Slavery & Abolition* 7 (1986): 3–24.

———. *Econocide: British Slavery in the Era of Abolition*. Pittsburgh: University of Pittsburgh Press, 1977.

———. *The Mighty Experiment: Free Labor versus Slavery in the Caribbean*. Oxford: Oxford University Press, 2004.

Dunkley, D. A. *Agency of the Enslaved: Jamaica and the Culture of Freedom in the Atlantic World*. New York: Lexington Books, 2013.

Dunn, Richard S. "The Demographic Contrast between Slave Life in Jamaica and Virginia." *Proceedings of the American Philosophical Society* 151 (2007): 43–60.

———. "'Dreadful Idlers' in the Cane Fields: The Slave Labor Pattern on a Jamaican Sugar Estate, 1762–1831." *Journal of Interdisciplinary History* 17 (1987): 795–822.

———. "The Story of Two Jamaican Slaves: Sarah Affir and Robert McAlpine of Mesopotamia Estate." In *West Indies Accounts: Essays on the History of the British Caribbean and the Atlantic Economy in Honour of Richard Sheridan*, edited by Roderick A. McDonald, 188–210. Kingston: University of the West Indies Press, 1996.

———. "Sugar Production and Slave Women in Jamaica." In *Cultivation and Culture: Labor and the Shaping of Slave Life in the Americas*, edited by Ira Berlin and Philip D. Morgan, 49–72. Charlottesville: University Press of Virginia, 1993.

Elkins, Stanley. *Slavery: A Problem in American Institutional and Intellectual Life*. Chicago: University of Chicago Press, 1959.

Eltis, David. *Economic Growth and the Ending of the Transatlantic Slave Trade*. Oxford: Oxford University Press, 1987.

———. "The Volume and Structure of the Transatlantic Slave Trade: A Reassessment." *William and Mary Quarterly* 58 (2001): 17–46.

———. *Voyages: The Trans-Atlantic Slave Trade Database*. http://www.slavevoyages.org/tast/database/search.faces. Accessed June 25, 2013.

Engerman, Stanley. "Pricing Freedom: Evaluating the Costs of Emancipation and of Manumission." In *Working Slavery, Pricing Freedom: Perspectives from the Caribbean, Africa, and the African Diaspora*, edited by Verene Shepherd, 273–302. New York: Palgrave, 2002.

———. "The Slave Trade and British Capital Formation in the 18th Century: A Comment on the Williams Thesis." *Business History Review* 46 (1972): 430–43.

Eudell, Demetrius L. *The Political Languages of Emancipation in the British Caribbean and the U.S. South*. Chapel Hill: University of North Carolina Press, 2001.

Fanon, Frantz. *Black Skin, White Masks*. Translated by Charles Lam Markmann. New York: Grove Press, 1967.

Fergus, Claudius. "The *Siete Partidas*: A Framework for Philanthropy and Coercion during the Amelioration Experiment in Trinidad, 1823–34." *Caribbean Studies* 36 (2008): 75–99.

Follett, Richard. "Heat, Sex, and Sugar: Pregnancy and Childbearing in the Slave Quarters." Journal of Family History *October* 28 (2003): 510–39.

Forster, Martin, and S. D. Smith. "Surviving Slavery: Mortality at Mesopotamia, a Jamaican Sugar Estate, 1762–1832." *Journal of the Royal Statistical Society* 174 (2011): 907–29.

Frazier, E. Franklin. *Folk Beliefs of the Southern Negro*. New York: Schocken, 1963.

Freyre, Gilberto. *The Masters and the Slaves*. Translated by Samuel Putnam. New York: Knopf, 1946.

Glasson, Travis. "'Baptism doth not bestow Freedom': Missionary Anglicanism, Slavery, and the Yorke-Talbot Opinion, 1701–30." *William and Mary Quarterly* 67 (2010): 279–318.

Gordon, Shirley C. *God Almighty, Make Me Free: Christianity in Pre-Emancipation Jamaica*. Bloomington: Indiana University Press, 1996.

———. *Our Cause for His Glory: Christianisation and Emancipation in Jamaica*. Mona: University of the West Indies Press, 1998.

Goveia, Elsa V. *Slave Society in the British Leeward Islands at the End of the Eighteenth Century*. Westport, CT: Greenwood Press, 1965.

Green, Cecilia A. "'A Civil Inconvenience'? The Vexed Question of Slave Marriage in the British West Indies." *Law and History Review* 25 (2007): 1–60.

Gregory, Ian. "Different Places, Different Stories: Infant Mortality Decline in England and Wales, 1851–1911." *Annals of the Association of American Geographers* 98 (2008): 773–94.

Gutman, Herbert G. *The Black Family in Slavery and Freedom, 1750–1925*. New York: Pantheon Books, 1976.

Hall, Catherine. *Civilising Subjects: Metropole and Colony in the English Imagination, 1830–1867*. Chicago: University of Chicago Press, 2002.

Hall, Douglas. "Absentee-Proprietorship in the British West Indies, to about 1850." *Jamaican Historical Review* 4 (1964): 15–35.

———. "The Apprenticeship System in Jamaica, 1834–1838." In *Apprenticeship and Emancipation*. Mona: Department of Extra-Mural Studies, University of the West Indies, 1987.

———. "The Diary of a Westmoreland Planter: Part 1. Thomas Thistlewood in the Vineyard, 1750–51." *Jamaica Journal* 21 (1988): 16–29.

———. "The Diary of a Westmoreland Planter: Conclusion. 'Above All Others: Phibbah.'" *Jamaica Journal* 22 (1989): 57–64.

———. *In Miserable Slavery: Thomas Thistlewood in Jamaica, 1750–86*. 2nd edition. Mona: University of the West Indies Press, 1999.

Hall, N. A. T. "Some Aspects of the 'Deficiency' Question in Jamaica in the Eighteenth Century." *Jamaica Journal* 7 (1973): 36–41.

Handler, Jerome S. "Diseases and Medical Disabilities of Enslaved Barbadians, from the Seventeenth Century to around 1838." *West Indian Medical Journal* 58 (2009): 33–49.

———. "Slave Medicine and Obeah in Barbados, circa 1650 to 1834." *NWIG: New West Indian Guide / Nieuwe West-Indische Gids* 74 (2000): 57–90.

Handler, Jerome S., and Robert S. Corruccini. "Weaning among West Indian Slaves: Historical and Bioanthropological Evidence from Barbados." *William and Mary Quarterly* 43 (1986): 111–17.

Handler, Jerome S., and Charlotte J. Frisbie. "Aspects of Slave Life in Barbados: Music and Its Cultural Context." *Caribbean Studies* 11 (1972): 5–46.

Handler, Jerome S., and JoAnn Jacoby. "Slave Names and Naming in Barbados, 1650–1830." *William and Mary Quarterly* 53 (1996): 685–728.

Harrison, Mark. *Medicine in an Age of Commerce and Empire: Britain and Its Tropical Colonies, 1600–1830*. Oxford: Oxford University Press, 2010.

Hart, Ansell. "Colour Prejudice in Jamaica." *Jamaica Journal* 4 (1970): 2–7.

Hawthorne, Walter. "'Being now, as it were, one family': Shipmate Bonding on the Slave Vessel *Emilia*, in Rio de Janeiro and throughout the Atlantic World." *Luso-Brazilian Review* 45 (2008): 53–77.

Henriques, Fernando. *Family and Colour in Jamaica*. London: MacGibbon and Kee, 1953.

Henry, Adina, and Thomas Rowe. "Anansi Stories." *Jamaica Journal* 16 (1983): 32–34.

Herskovits, Melville J. *The Myth of the Negro Past*. New York: Harper and Brothers, 1941.

Heuman, Gad. *Between Black and White: Race, Politics, and the Free Coloreds in Jamaica, 1792–1865*. Westport, CT: Greenwood Press, 1981.

———. "White over Brown over Black: The Free Coloured in Jamaican Society during Slavery and after Emancipation." *Journal of Caribbean History* 14 (1981): 46–68.

Heywood, Colin. *A History of Childhood: Children and Childhood in the West from Medieval to Modern Times*. Cambridge, UK: Polity Press, 2001.

Higman, B. W. "African and Creole Slave Family Patterns in Trinidad." *Journal of Family History* 3 (1978): 163–80.

———. *Enslaved Population and Economy in Jamaica, 1807–1834*. Mona: University of the West Indies Press, 1995.

———. "Household Structure and Fertility on Jamaican Slave Plantations: A Nineteenth-Century Example." *Population Studies* 27 (1973): 527–50.

———. "The Internal Economy of Jamaican Pens, 1760–1890." *Social and Economic Studies* 38 (1989): 61–86.

———. *Jamaica Surveyed: Plantation Maps and Plans of the Eighteenth and Nineteenth Centuries*. Mona: University of the West Indies Press, 2001.

———. *Montpelier Jamaica: A Plantation Community in Slavery and Freedom, 1739–1912*. Mona: University of the West Indies Press, 1998.

———. *Plantation Jamaica, 1750–1850: Capital and Control in a Colonial Economy*. Kingston: University of the West Indies Press, 2008.

———. "The Slave Family and Household in the British West Indies, 1800–1834." *Journal of Interdisciplinary History* 6 (1975): 261–87.

———. *Slave Population and Economy, 1807–1834*. Mona: University of the West Indies Press, 1995.

———. "The West India Interest in Parliament, 1807–1833." *Historical Studies* 13 (1967): 1–19.

Hogg, Peter C. *The African Slave Trade and Its Suppression: A Classified and Annotated Bibliography of Books, Pamphlets and Periodical Articles*. London: Frank Cass, 1973.

Holloway, Joseph E., ed. *Africanisms in American Culture*. Bloomington: Indiana University Press, 1991.

Holt, Thomas C. "Explaining Abolition." *Journal of Social History* 24 (1990): 371–78.

———. *The Problem of Freedom: Race, Labor, and Politics in Jamaica and Britain, 1832–1938*. Baltimore: Johns Hopkins University Press, 1992.

Hurwitz, Samuel J., and Edith F. Hurwitz. "A Token of Freedom: Private Bill Legislation for Free Negroes in Eighteenth-Century Jamaica." *William and Mary Quarterly* 24 (1967): 423–31.

James, Cynthia. "From Orature to Literature in Jamaican and Trinidadian Children's Folk Traditions." *Children's Literature Association Quarterly* 30 (2005): 164–78.

Jennings, Thelma. "'Us Colored Women Had to Go through A Plenty': Sexual Exploitation of African-American Slave women." *Journal of Women's History* 1 (1990): 45–74.

Jensen, Niklas Thode. *For the Health of the Enslaved: Slaves, Medicine, and Power in the Danish West Indies, 1803–1848*. Copenhagen: Museum Tusculanum Press of the University of Copenhagen, 2011.

Jones, Cecily. "'If this be living I'd rather be dead': Enslaved Youth, Agency, and

Resistance on an Eighteenth Century Jamaican Estate." *History of the Family* 12 (2007): 92–103.

Jordan, Winthrop. "American Chiaroscuro: The Status and Definition of Mulattoes in the British Colonies." *William and Mary Quarterly* 19 (1962): 183–200.

Kale, Madhavi. *Fragments of Empire: Capital, Slavery, and Indian Indentured Labor Migration in the British Caribbean.* Philadelphia: University of Pennsylvania Press, 1998.

Keating-Miller, Jennifer, and Michael Given. *Explorations of Affiliation: Irish Indentured Servitude in the English West Indies.* Rock Hill, SC: Winthrop University Press, 2008.

Kenny, Gale L. *Contentious Liberties: American Abolitionists in Post-Emancipation Jamaica, 1834–1866.* Athens: University of Georgia Press, 2010.

Kerr-Ritchie, Jeffrey R. *Rights of August First: Emancipation Day in the Black Atlantic.* Baton Rouge: Louisiana State University Press, 2007.

King, Ruby Hope. *Education in the Caribbean: Historical Perspectives.* Mona: Faculty of Education, University of the West Indies, 1987.

King, Wilma. *Stolen Childhood: Slave Youth in Nineteenth-Century America.* Bloomington: Indiana University Press, 1995.

Kiple, Kenneth F. *The Caribbean Slave: A Biological History.* Cambridge, UK: Cambridge University Press, 1984.

———. "The Nutritional Link with Slave Infant and Child Mortality in Brazil." *Hispanic American Historical Review* 69 (1989): 677–90.

Kleijwegt, Marc, ed. *The Faces of Freedom: The Manumission and Emancipation of Slaves in Old World and New World Slavery.* Leiden: Brill Academic, 2006.

Klein, Herbert S. "The English Slave Trade to Jamaica, 1782–1808." *Economic History Review* 31 (1978): 25–45.

Klein, Herbert S., and Stanley Engerman. "Fertility Differentials between Slaves in the United States and the British West Indies: A Note on Lactation Practices and Their Possible Implications." *William and Mary Quarterly* 35 (1978): 357–74.

Knight, Franklin W., ed. *General History of the Caribbean.* Vol. 3: *The Slave Societies of the Caribbean.* London: UNESCO, 1997.

Konadu, Kwasi. *The Akan Diaspora in the Americas.* Oxford: Oxford University Press, 2010.

Kouwenberg, Silvia. "Africans in Early English Jamaica (1655–1700): The Akan-Dominance Myth." In *Freedom: Retrospective and Prospective,* edited by Swithon R. Wilmot, 32–44. Kingston, Jamaica: Ian Randle, 2009.

Lalla, Barbara, and Jean D'Costa. *Language in Exile: Three Hundred Years of Jamaican Creole.* Birmingham: University of Alabama Press, 2009.

Lamur, Humphrey E. "The Slave Family in Colonial 19th-Century Suriname." *Journal of Black Studies* 23 (1993): 371–81.

Linyard, Fred. "The Moravians in Jamaica from the Beginning of Emancipation, 1754 to 1838." *Jamaica Journal* 3 (1969): 7–11.

Livesay, Daniel. "All in the Family: Mixed-Race Jamaicans and Their Imperial Networks in the Eighteenth Century." In *(Re)Figuring Human Enslavement: Images of Power, Violence and Resistance*, edited by Ulrich Pallua, Adrian Knapp, and Andreas Exenberger, 149–66. Innsbruck, Austria: Innsbruck University Press, 2009.

———. "The Decline of Jamaica's Interracial Households and the Fall of the Planter Class, 1733–1823." *Atlantic Studies* 9 (2012): 107–23.

LoGerfo, James W. "Sir William Dolben and 'The Cause of Humanity': The Passage of the Slave Trade Regulation Act of 1788." *Eighteenth-Century Studies* 6 (1973): 431–51.

Look Lai, Walton. *Indentured Labor, Caribbean Sugar: Chinese and Indian Migrants to the British West Indies, 1838–1918*. Baltimore: Johns Hopkins University Press, 1993.

Luster, Robert E. *The Amelioration of the Slaves in the British Empire, 1790–1833*. New York: Peter Lang, 1995.

Lutz, Jessie G. "Chinese Emigrants, Indentured Workers, and Christianity in the West Indies, British Guiana and Hawaii." *Caribbean Studies* 37 (2009): 133–54.

Maclean, Isabel Cranstoun. *Children of Jamaica*. Edinburgh: Oliphant, Anderson and Ferrier, 1910.

Mair, Lucille Mathurin. *Women Field Workers in Jamaica during Slavery*. Mona: Department of History, University of the West Indies, 1987.

Marshall, Emily Zoebel. "Anansi, Eshu, and Legba: Slave Resistance and the West African Trickster." In *Human Bondage in the Cultural Contact Zone: Transdisciplinary Perspectives on Slavery and Its Discourses*, edited by Raphael Hörmann and Gesa Mackenthun, 171–86. Münster: Waxmann, 2010.

———. *Anansi's Journey: A Story of Jamaican Cultural Resistance*. Kingston: University of the West Indies Press, 2012.

Mathewson, R. Duncan. "Archaeological Analysis of Material Culture as a Reflection of Subcultural Differentiation in the 18th Century Jamaica." In *Eighteenth Century Florida and the Caribbean*, edited by Samuel Proctor, 75–87. Gainesville: University Presses of Florida, 1976.

Matthews, Gelien. *Caribbean Slave Revolts and the British Abolitionist Movement*. Baton Rouge: Louisiana State University Press, 2013.

McDonald, Roderick A. *The Economy and Material Culture of Slaves: Goods and Chattels on the Sugar Plantations of Jamaica and Louisiana*. Baton Rouge: Louisiana State University Press, 1993.

———. "Measuring the British Slave Trade to Jamaica, 1789–1808: A Comment." *Economic History Review* 33 (1980): 253–58.

McLewin, Philip J. *Power and Economic Change: The Response to Emancipation in Jamaica and British Guiana, 1840–1865*. New York: Garland, 1987.

Meyers, Allan D. "West African Tradition in the Decoration of Colonial Jamaican Folk Pottery." *International Journal of Historical Archaeology* 3 (1999): 201–23.

Mintz, Sidney W., and Richard Price. *The Birth of African-American Culture: An Anthropological Perspective.* Boston: Beacon Press, 1992.

Moitt, Bernard. *Women and Slavery in the French Antilles, 1635–1848.* Urbana: Indiana University Press, 2001.

Morgan, Jennifer L. *Laboring Women: Reproduction and Gender in New World Slavery.* Philadelphia: University of Pennsylvania Press, 2004.

Morgan, Kenneth. "Slave Women and Reproduction in Jamaica, 1776–1834." *History* 91 (2006): 231–53.

Morrissey, Marietta. *Slave Women in the New World: Gender Stratification in the Caribbean.* Lawrence: University Press of Kansas, 1989.

Moumouni, Abdou. *Education in Africa.* London: Andre Deutsch, 1968.

Mouser, Bruce L. *A Slaving Voyage to Africa and Jamaica: The Log of the Sundown, 1793–1794.* Bloomington: Indiana University Press, 2002.

Mullin, Michael. *Africa in America: Slave Acculturation and Resistance in the American South and the British Caribbean, 1736–1831.* Urbana: University of Illinois Press, 1992.

Munro, Martin. "Slaves to the Rhythm: The Rhythmic Evolution of Plantation Societies." *Contemporary French and Francophone Studies* 15 (2011): 27–35.

Murdoch, H. Adlai. "A Legacy of Trauma: Caribbean Slavery, Race, Class, and Contemporary Identity in *Abeng*." *Research in African Literatures* 40 (2009): 65–88.

Murray, Deryck. "Three Worships, an Old Warlock and Many Lawless Forces: The Court Trial of an African Doctor Who Practised 'Obeah to Cure' in Early Nineteenth Century Jamaica." *Journal of Southern African Studies* 33 (2007): 811–28.

Newman, Brooke N. "Contesting 'Black' Liberty and Subjecthood in the Anglophone Caribbean, 1730s–1780s." *Slavery & Abolition* 32 (2011): 169–83.

———. "Gender, Sexuality and the Formation of Racial Identities in the Eighteenth-Century Anglo-Caribbean World." *Gender and History* 22 (2010): 585–602.

Newton, Melanie J. "Freedom's Prisons: Incarceration, Emancipation, and Modernity in No Bond but the Law." *Small Axe* 15 (2011): 164–75.

Okpewho, Isidore, Carole Boyce Davies, and Ali A. Mazrui, eds. *The African Diaspora: African Origins and New World Identities.* Bloomington: Indiana University Press, 2001.

Olwig, Karen Fog. "Finding a Place for the Slave Family: Historical Anthropological Perspectives." *Folk* 23 (1981): 345–58.

Omolewa, Michael. "Traditional African Modes of Education: Their Relevance in the Modern World." *International Review of Education* 53 (2007): 593–612.

O'Shaughnessy, Andrew J. *An Empire Divided: The American Revolution and the British Caribbean.* Philadelphia: University of Pennsylvania Press, 2000.

———. "The Formation of a Commercial Lobby: The West India Interest, British Colonial Policy and the American Revolution." *Historical Journal* 40 (1997): 71–95.

The Oxford History of the British Empire: The Eighteenth Century. Oxford: Oxford University Press, 1998.

Palmer, Colin A. *Africa in the Making of the Caribbean: The Formative Years*. Mona: Department of History, University of the West Indies, 1996.

Pares, Richard. *A West India Fortune*. London: Longmans, Green, 1950.

Paton, Diana. *No Bond but the Law: Punishment, Race, and Gender in Jamaican State Formation, 1780–1870*. Durham, NC: Duke University Press, 2004.

Paton, Diana, and Pamela Scully. *Gender and Slave Emancipation in the Atlantic World*. Durham, NC: Duke University Press, 2005.

Patterson, Orlando. "From Endo-deme to Matri-deme: An Interpretation of the Development of Kinship and Social Organization among the Slaves of Jamaica, 1655–1830." In *Eighteenth Century Florida and the Caribbean*, edited by Samuel Proctor, 50–59. Gainesville: University Presses of Florida, 1976.

———. *The Sociology of Slavery: An Analysis of the Origins, Development, and Structure of Negro Slave Society in Jamaica*. London: Associated University Presses, 1967.

Payne-Jackson, Arvilla, and Mervyn C. Alleyne. *Jamaican Folk Medicine: A Source of Healing*. Mona: University of West Indies Press, 2004.

Pemberton, Rita, and Brinsley Samaroo, eds. "Eric Williams: Images of His Life." Special issue of *Caribbean Issues* 8.1 (1998).

Pemberton, Rita, and Brinsley Samaroo, eds. "Eric Williams: Images of His Life." Special issue of *Caribbean Issues* 8.2 (1999).

Penson, Lillian M. "The London West India Interest in the Eighteenth Century." *English Historical Review* 36 (1921): 373–92.

Petley, Christer. "'Legitimacy' and Social Boundaries: Free People of Colour and the Social Order in Jamaican Slave Society." *Social History* 30 (2005): 481–98.

———. *Slaveholders in Jamaica: Colonial Society and Culture during the Era of Abolition*. London: Pickering and Chatto, 2009.

Pigou, Elizabeth. "A Note on Afro-Jamaican Beliefs and Rituals." *Jamaica Journal* 20 (1987): 23–26.

Plumb, J. H. "The New World of Children in Eighteenth-Century England." *Past and Present* 67 (1975): 64–95.

Pollack, Linda, ed. *A Lasting Relationship: Parents and Children over Three Centuries*. Hanover, NH: University Press of New England, 1987.

Purchas-Tulloch, J. A. "Jamaica Anansi: A Survivor of African Oral Tradition." Ph.D. dissertation, Howard University, 1976.

Reid, Ahmed, and David B. Ryden. "Sugar, Land Markets, and the Williams Thesis: Evidence from Jamaica's Property Sales, 1750–1810." *Slavery & Abolition* 34 (2013): 401–24.

Riley, James C. *Poverty and Life Expectancy: The Jamaican Paradox*. Cambridge, UK: Cambridge University Press, 2005.

Riviere, W. Emanuel. "Labour Shortage in the British West Indies after Emancipation." *Journal of Caribbean History* 4 (1972): 1–30.

Roberts, G. W. *The Population of Jamaica*. Cambridge, UK: Published for the Conservation Foundation at the University Press, 1957.

Roberts, George W. "A Life Table for a West Indian Enslaved Population." *Population Studies* 5 (1951–52): 238–43.

Roberts, Justin. *Slavery and the Enlightenment in the British Atlantic, 1750–1807*. Cambridge, UK: Cambridge University Press, 2013.

Robertson, James. "An Essay Concerning Slavery: A Mid-Eighteenth-Century Analysis from Jamaica." *Slavery & Abolition* 33 (2012): 65–85.

———. *Gone Is the Ancient Glory: Spanish Town, Jamaica, 1534–2000*. Kingston, Jamaica: Ian Randle, 2005.

Rooke, Patricia T. "A Scramble for Souls: The Impact of the Negro Education Grant on Evangelical Missionaries in the British West Indies." *History of Education Quarterly* 21 (1981): 429–47.

Russell, Horace. "The Emergence of the Christian Black: The Making of a Stereotype." *Jamaican Journal* 16 (1983): 51–58.

Salih, Sarah. *Representing Mixed Race in Jamaica and England from the Abolition Era to the Present*. New York: Routledge, 2010.

Saunders, Paula V. "Free and Enslaved African Communities in Buff Bay, Jamaica: Daily Life, Resistance, and Kinship, 1750–1834." Ph.D. dissertation, University of Texas, 2004.

Schuler, Monica. *"Alas, Alas, Kongo": A Social History of Indentured African Immigration into Jamaica, 1841–1865*. Baltimore: Johns Hopkins University Press, 1980.

Schwartz, Marie Jenkins. *Born in Bondage: Growing Up Enslaved in the Antebellum South*. Cambridge, MA: Harvard University Press, 2000.

Senior, Carl. "The *Robert Kerr* Emigrants: 'Irish Slaves for Jamaica.'" *Jamaica Journal* 12 (1978): 104–16.

Senior, Olive. *A–Z of Jamaican Heritage*. 3rd edition. Kingston, Jamaica: Heinemann Educational Books, Gleaner, 1985.

Shayt, David H. "Stairway to Redemption: America's Encounter with the British Prison Treadmill." *Technology and Culture* 30 (1989): 908–38.

Shepherd, Verene A. "The Apprenticeship Experience on Jamaican Livestock Pens, 1834–1838." *Jamaica Journal* 22 (1989): 48–55.

———. "Ethnicity, Colour, and Gender in the Experiences of Enslaved Women on Non-Sugar Properties in Jamaica." In *Trans-Atlantic Dimensions of Ethnicity in the African Diaspora*, edited by Paul E. Lovejoy and David V. Trotman, 195–217. London: Continuum, 2003.

———. *Livestock, Sugar and Slavery: Contested Terrain in Colonial Jamaica*. Kingston, Jamaica: Ian Randle, 2009.

———. *Transients to Settlers: The Experience of Indians in Jamaica, 1845–1950*. Leeds, UK: Peepal Tree, University of Warwick Press, 1994.

Sheridan, Richard B. *Doctors and Slaves: A Medical and Demographic History of Slavery in the British West Indies, 1680–1834*. Cambridge, UK: Cambridge University Press, 1985.

———. "Mortality and the Medical Treatment of Slaves in the British West Indies." In *Caribbean Slave Society and Economy: A Student Reader*, edited by Hilary Beckles and Verene Shepherd, 197–208. New York: New Press, 1991.

———. "Slave Medicine in Jamaica: Thomas Thistlewood's 'Receipts for a Physick,' 1750–1786." *Jamaican Historical Review* 17 (1991): 1–18.

———. "The Wealth of Jamaica in the Eighteenth Century." *Economic History Review* 18 (1965): 292–311.

Sio, Arnold A. "Marginality and Free Coloured Identity in Caribbean Slave Society." *Slavery & Abolition* 8 (1987): 166–82.

Small, Stephen. "Racial Group Boundaries and Identities: People of 'Mixed Race' in Slavery across the Americas." *Slavery & Abolition* 15 (1994): 17–37.

Stampp, Kenneth. *The Peculiar Institution: Slavery in the Ante-Bellum South*. New York: Knopf, 1967.

Stark, David M. "Discovering the Invisible Puerto Rican Slave Family: Demographic Evidence from the Eighteenth Century." *Journal of Family History* 21 (1996): 395–418.

Steckel, Richard. "Diets versus Diseases: The Anthropometries of Enslaved Children: A Reply." *Journal of Economic History* 60 (2000): 247–59.

———. "A Peculiar Population: The Nutrition, Health, and Mortality of American Slaves from Childhood to Maturity." *Journal of Economic History* 46 (1986): 721–41.

Stewart, Dianne M. *Three Eyes for the Journey: The African Dimensions of the Jamaican Religious Experience*. Oxford: Oxford University Press, 2005.

Stewart, Robert J. *Religion and Society in Post-Emancipation Jamaica*. Knoxville: University of Tennessee Press, 1992.

Stoler, Ann Laura. *Carnal Knowledge and Imperial Power: Race and the Intimate in Colonial Rule*. Berkeley: University of California Press, 2002.

Stonequist, Everett V. *The Marginal Man: A Study in Personality and Culture Conflict*. New York: Russell and Russell, 1961.

Sturtz, Linda L. "The 'Dim Duke' and Duchess Chandos: Gender and Power in Jamaican Plantation Management—A Case Study or, A Different Story of 'A Man [and His Wife] from a Place Called Hope.'" *Revista / Review Interameriana* 29 (1999). http://cai.sg.inter.edu/revista-ciscla/volume29/sturtz.html. Accessed January 11, 2014.

Sweet, James H. *Recreating Africa: Culture, Kinship, and Religion in the African-Portuguese World, 1441–1770*. Chapel Hill: University of North Carolina Press, 2003.

Tadman, Michael. "The Demographic Cost of Sugar: Debates on Slave Societies and Natural Increase in the Americas." *American Historical Review* 105 (2000): 1534–75.

Tanna, Laura. "African Retentions: Yoruba and Kikongo Songs in Jamaica." *Jamaica Journal* 16 (1983): 47–52.

———. "Anansi: Jamaica's Trickster Hero." *Jamaica Journal* 16 (1983): 20–30.

———. *Jamaican Folk Tales and Oral Histories*. Kingston: Institute of Jamaica, 1984.

Thornton, Amanda. "Coerced Care: Thomas Thistlewood's Account of Medical Practice on Enslaved Populations in Colonial Jamaica, 1751–1786." *Slavery & Abolition* 32 (2011): 535–59.

Tortello, R. "The Magical Spider-man: The Metamorphoses of Bredda Anansi." Ph.D. dissertation, Harvard University, 1991.

Turner, Mary. "The 11 O'Clock Flog: Women, Work and Labour Law in the British Caribbean." *Slavery & Abolition* 20 (1999): 38–58.

———. *Slaves and Missionaries: The Disintegration of Jamaican Slave Society, 1787–1834*. Mona: University of the West Indies Press, 1998.

Turner, Sasha. "Home-grown Slaves: Women, Reproduction, and the Abolition of the Slave Trade, Jamaica 1788–1807." *Journal of Women's History* 23.3 (2011): 39–62.

Van der Berghe, Pierre. *Race and Racism: A Comparative Perspective*. New York: John Wiley and Sons, 1967.

Vasconcellos, Colleen. "From Chattel to Breeding Wenches: Girlhood in a Jamaican Slave Community." In *Girlhood: A Global History*, edited by Jennifer Hillman Helgren and Colleen A. Vasconcellos, 325–43. New Brunswick, NJ: Rutgers University Press, 2010.

Ward, J. R. *British West Indian Slavery, 1750–1834: The Process of Amelioration*. Oxford: Oxford University Press, 1988.

Warner-Lewis, Maureen. *Archibald Monteith: Igbo, Jamaica, Moravian*. Kingston: University of the West Indies Press, 2007.

———. *Central Africa in the Caribbean: Transcending Time, Transforming Cultures*. Mona: University of West Indies Press, 2003.

———. "The Character of African-Jamaican Culture." In *Jamaica in Slavery and Freedom: History, Heritage, and Culture*, edited by Kathleen E. A. Monteith and Glen Richards, 89–114. Mona: University of the West Indies Press, 2002.

Welch, Pedro. "The Slave Family in the Urban Context: Views from Bridgetown, Barbados, 1789–1816." *Journal of Caribbean History* 29 (1995): 11–24.

Wickstrom, Stefanie. "The Politics of Forbidden Liaisons: Civilization, Miscegenation, and Other Perversions." *Frontiers: A Journal of Women Studies* 26 (2005): 168–98.

Williams, Eric. *Capitalism and Slavery*. Chapel Hill: University of North Carolina Press, 1944.

Wilmot, Swithin R., ed. *Adjustments to Emancipation in Jamaica.* Mona: Department of History, University of the West Indies, 1994.

———. "Not 'Full Free': The Ex-Slaves and the Apprenticeship System in Jamaica, 1834–1838." *Jamaica Journal* 17 (1984): 2–10.

Wilson, Andrew R., ed. *The Chinese in the Caribbean.* Princeton, NJ: Markus Wiener, 2004.

Winter, Sylvia. "Lady Nugent's Journal." *Jamaica Journal* 1 (1967): 23–34.

Wright, Philip. *Knibb, "the Notorious": The Slaves' Missionary 1803–1845.* London: Sidgwick and Jackson, 1973.

Yarbrough, Fay A. "Power, Perception, and Interracial Sex: Former Slaves Recall a Multiracial South." *Journal of Southern History* 71 (2005): 559–88.

Yun, Lisa. *The Coolie Speaks: Chinese Indentured Laborers and African Slaves in Cuba.* Philadelphia: Temple University Press, 2008.

Zelizer, Viviana. *Pricing the Priceless Child: The Changing Social Value of Children.* 2nd edition. Princeton, NJ: Princeton University Press, 1994.

Index

Early American Places

On Slavery's Border: Missouri's Small Slaveholding Households, 1815–1865
by Diane Mutti Burke

Sounding America: Identity and the Music Culture of the Lower Mississippi River Valley, 1800–1860
by Ann Ostendorf

The Year of the Lash: Free People of Color in Cuba and the Nineteenth-Century Atlantic World
by Michele Reid-Vazquez

Ordinary Lives in the Early Caribbean: Religion, Colonial Competition, and the Politics Of Profit
by Kirsten Block

Creolization and Contraband: Curaçao in the Early Modern Atlantic World
by Linda M. Rupert

An Empire of Small Places: Mapping the Southeastern Anglo-Indian Trade, 1732–1795
by Robert Paulett

Everyday Life in the Early English Caribbean: Irish, Africans, and the Construction of Difference
by Jenny Shaw

Natchez Country: Indians, Colonists, and the Landscapes of Race in French Louisiana
by George Edward Milne

Slavery, Childhood, and Abolition in Jamaica, 1788–1838
by Colleen A. Vasconcellos